PREFACE

New Voices: Contemporary Poetry from the United States and its companion anthology *The New North: Contemporary Poetry from Northern Ireland* constitute an unusual literary enterprise. These complementary volumes—one published in Belfast by Irish Pages and the other in the United States by Wake Forest University Press—introduce the contemporary poetry of each country to readers in the other nation. This important literary exchange offers a distinguished selection of poetry to cultivate new audiences and deepen cultural understanding between our two countries—so famously separated by "the barrier of a common language."

The production of these books required an enormous investment of time, energy, and expertise. Many poets, editors, and arts administrators have collaborated across great distances to make them possible. In particular, I would like to commend the editor, H. L. Hix, for his effective leadership throughout the process. I also want to thank our partners at the Arts Council of Northern Ireland, Rosemary Kelly, Chairman, and Roisín McDonough, Chief Executive, as well as Director of Arts Support, Philip Hammond. *New Voices* is an exceptionally handsome and well crafted volume. My sincere appreciation goes to Chris Agee, Editor of Irish Pages, for his care and attention in publishing this book.

There can be little doubt that over the past forty years Northern Ireland has enjoyed something of a golden age of poetry. As literary history suggests, superior poets tend to emerge in clusters since human talents seem to develop best in proximity to other sympathetic talents. The emergence of poets like Seamus Heaney, Derek Mahon, Michael

Longley, Ciaran Carson, and Paul Muldoon, in the compact area of only six contiguous counties, displays a density of artistic talent that any nation might envy.

By comparison, the U.S. literary scene must seem sprawling, vast, and confoundingly various. There has probably never been a nation with so many poets as contemporary America, nor a culture in which they have so little in common, especially among the younger generation. There is no single stylistic or thematic direction that typifies the best work of this new cohort. These younger poets write in a wide range of modes from traditional to experimental. Metered poetry and free verse coexist, as do lyrical, narrative, and discursive verse. Identity poetry, which puts the personal and cultural background of the writer at the center of the work, still flourishes—but so, too, do the less subjective styles of narrative verse and the deliberately objectified modes of postmodernism.

If there is no identifiable mainstream for new poetry in the United States, then the importance of these poets is not their collective allegiances, but rather their individual distinction. The astute and intrepid editor of this anthology, H. L. Hix, has presented us with the enormous, imaginative variety of contemporary American poetry. Turning the pages of this volume, the reader will not be able to predict what the next poet will offer—except perhaps energy and surprise.

—DANA GIOIA

Chairman

National Endowment for the Arts

INTRODUCTION

About contemporary poetry the most astonishing fact is how much there is, and how much of it merits attention. Ezra Pound's globalizing impulse alerted us to the plethora of poetry from other shores and in other languages, but even confining oneself to English-language poetry written by Americans, so many worthy poets are writing so much valid and various poetry that one might speculate—or fantasize —about a new renaissance. Dante's decision to write his *Divine Comedy* in the vernacular instead of in Latin, the language of the learned, foreshadowed his country's producing, in addition to his fellow poets Petrarch and Boccaccio, such revolutionary artists and scientists as Michelangelo and Leonardo and Galileo and Giordano Bruno. One poet sang in the language the people spoke, and soon we were orbiting the sun, god's outstretched finger mere inches from ours.

Contemporary poetic assertion of the vernacular occurs not, like Dante's, as a change of language per se—there being no language of the learned now to leave—but as a multiplicity of voices from previously slighted segments of the citizenry (women, persons of color), still a defiance of the tongue of the few by the tongue of the many, but this time as vernaculars, plural, instead of a single vernacular. Why not hope we are witnessing the cultural equivalent of Dante's magisterial magnum opus, that single work at the waist of the hourglass through which European culture passed? The magnitude of Dante's achievement had to take the form of quantity and influence: to go from one language to another demanded a single, big book that absorbed all that preceded it and colored all that followed. But the magnitude of contemporary poetic achievement expresses itself instead as number and momentum: to hear the cacophony of previously muffled voices demands not a single book but a multitude of books, not one wash that colors the horizon but plentiful pointillist dots that merge into hue.

Change of language asks for translation, variousness of voices for anthologizing. For a translator, the necessary partiality of any success enforces a modesty before the task, and so with an anthologist. The translator must try, as one tries with metaphor, to overcome unlikeness: how transfer a poem that depends on the characteristics of one language into a language with different characteristics? The anthologist must try, as one tries with synecdoche, to overcome incompletion: how present a whole through a few parts? But for the anthologist as for the translator, the obligatory apology for the inadequacy of the means to the object implies praise of the object. An anthology is impossible when the field it represents is ample and important, but is *needed* just when and precisely because the field is ample and important. In the disclaimers that follow, then, I hope the reader will hear praise of the ample and important field of contemporary American poetry.

Though the lament I hear most often uttered about contemporary American poetry is its uniformity, in fact its most notable feature, I have just tried to suggest, is its plurality. Within the parameters assigned me (thirty poets, three poems each, no poet born before 1965), I have tried to suggest that plurality. Suggest, not exhaust. As an antidote to the assumption that plurality entails isolation and incongruity, I have begun the collection with one poem from a previous generation and ended it with another, to insinuate by the first a continuity through the plurality that follows it, and by the second to insinuate that the mysterious power of poetry is not limited to poetry of one kind or school.

Marina Tsvetaeva argued against "liking" as the measure of a poem, and though my tastes are, I hope, eclectic, they are also limited, so I have tried, not to eliminate my tastes, but to subordinate them to the anthology's pluralist agenda. This collection includes many poets whose work I like, but instead of simply choosing the thirty young poets whose work I like most I have tried to nod toward a breadth and range that exceeds any one person's tastes. This anthology is not an act of advocacy for the individual selections, but a suggestion that the United States may model global citizenship—responsibility and mutuality in the presence of difference—more robustly in its poetry than in its foreign policy.

I have tried in this anthology to represent a range of stylistic practices, various ways of perceiving poetry's relationship to public life, a stew of authorial identities (race, gender, ethnicity, class). I have included poets who already are widely anthologized, publishing with large presses, and receiving major prizes, along with poets whose reputations do not yet match the quality of their work.

I hope this anthology will fulfill the best spirit of cultural exchange between the United States and Northern Ireland, introducing its readers to a few of the many exciting voices in American poetry today, and that in doing so it will "go to school to youth," as Robert Frost's poem urges, "to learn the future."

—H. L. HIX

WILLIAM STAFFORD

[1914–1993]

ASK ME

Some time when the river is ice ask me
mistakes I have made. Ask me whether
what I have done is my life. Others
have come in their slow way into
my thought, and some have tried to help
or to hurt: ask me what difference
their strongest love or hate has made.

I will listen to what you say.
You and I can turn and look
at the silent river and wait. We know
the current is there, hidden; and there
are comings and goings from miles away
that hold the stillness exactly before us.
What the river says, that is what I say.

SHERMAN ALEXIE

[B. 1966]

EVOLUTION

Buffalo Bill opens a pawn shop on the reservation
right across the border from the liquor store
and he stays open 24 hours a day, 7 days a week

and the Indians come running in with jewelry
television sets, a VCR, a full-length beaded buckskin outfit
it took Inez Muse 12 years to finish. Buffalo Bill

takes everything the Indians have to offer, keeps it
all catalogued and filed in a storage room. The Indians
pawn their hands, saving the thumbs for last, they pawn

their skeletons, falling endlessly from the skin
and when the last Indian has pawned everything
but his heart, Buffalo Bill takes that for twenty bucks

closes up the pawn shop, paints a new sign over the old
calls his venture THE MUSEUM OF NATIVE AMERICAN CULTURES
charges the Indians five bucks a head to enter.

ON THE AMTRAK FROM BOSTON
TO NEW YORK CITY

The white woman across the aisle from me says, "Look,
look at all the history, that house
on the hill there is over two hundred years old,"
as she points out the window past me

into what she has been taught. I have learned
little more about American history during my few days
back East than what I expected and far less
of what we should all know of the tribal stories

whose architecture is 15,000 years older
than the corners of the house that sits
museumed on the hill. "Walden Pond,"
the woman on the train asks, "Did you see Walden Pond?"

and I don't have a cruel enough heart to break
her own by telling her there are five Walden Ponds
on my little reservation out West
and at least a hundred more surrounding Spokane,

the city I pretend to call my home. "Listen,"
I could have told her. "I don't give a shit
about Walden. I know the Indians were living stories
around that pond before Walden's grandparents were born

and before his grandparents' grandparents were born.
I'm tired of hearing about Don-fucking-Henley saving it, too,
because that's redundant. If Don Henley's brothers and sisters
and mothers and fathers hadn't come here in the first place

then nothing would need to be saved."
But I didn't say a word to the woman about Walden
Pond because she smiled so much and seemed delighted
that I thought to bring her an orange juice

back from the food car. I respect elders
of every color. All I really did was eat
my tasteless sandwich, drink my Diet Pepsi
and nod my head whenever the woman pointed out

another little piece of her country's history
while I, as all Indians have done
since this war began, made plans
for what I would do and say the next time

somebody from the enemy thought I was one of their own.

THE POWWOW AT THE END OF THE WORLD

I am told by many of you that I must forgive and so I shall
after an Indian woman puts her shoulder to the Grand Coulee Dam
and topples it. I am told by many of you that I must forgive

and so I shall after the floodwaters burst each successive dam
downriver from the Grand Coulee. I am told by many of you
that I must forgive and so I shall after the floodwaters find
their way to the mouth of the Columbia River as it enters the Pacific
and causes all of it to rise. I am told by many of you that I must forgive
and so I shall after the first drop of floodwater is swallowed by that salmon
waiting in the Pacific. I am told by many of you that I must forgive and so I shall
after that salmon swims upstream, through the mouth of the Columbia
and then past the flooded cities, broken dams and abandoned reactors
of Hanford. I am told by many of you that I must forgive and so I shall
after that salmon swims through the mouth of the Spokane River
as it meets the Columbia, then upstream, until it arrives
in the shallows of a secret bay on the reservation where I wait alone.
I am told by many of you that I must forgive and so I shall after
that salmon leaps into the night air above the water, throws
a lightning bolt at the brush near my feet, and starts the fire
which will lead all of the lost Indians home. I am told
by many of you that I must forgive and so I shall
after we Indians have gathered around the fire with that salmon
who has three stories it must tell before sunrise: one story will teach us
how to pray; another story will make us laugh for hours;
the third story will give us reason to dance. I am told by many
of you that I must forgive and so I shall when I am dancing
with my tribe during the powwow at the end of the world.

JULIANA SPAHR

[B. 1966]

GATHERING: PALOLO STREAM

A place allows certain things.

A place allows certain things
and certain of we of a specific
place have certain rights.

∎

To go to the stream is a right for
certain people.

To go, to gather.

∎

The stream is a right.

It is a place for gathering.

A place for gathering āholehole

or for gathering guava, mīkana,
mai'a

or for gathering palapalai.

∎

The stream is many things.

Is busted television and niu.

Is rat and kī.

Is mongoose and freshwater.

Is ʻawa and kukui.

                              ▪

Beside the stream is a parking lot.

Yet there is no road into the
parking lot.

                              ▪

The parking lot is surrounded by
buildings on two sides

by a fence on a third

by a stream on the fourth.

                              ▪

Where the road once was is now
a parking lot for a rental space
business.

The rental space business has
surrounded their parking lot with
a high fence.

The fence gets locked at night.

∎

This is about how certain of we
have rights on paper yet not in
place.

Certain of we have a right to a
gathering of the stream.

∎

While the parking lot is unused,

while the stream is rich and full,

the parking lot represents the
general feeling of the space.

There is the parking lot of
limited space

the parking lot of owned by
certain of we

the parking lot of no possibility of
use

the parking lot of being unable to
park

the parking lot of growing from
the stream of gathering's freshness
of water

the parking lot beneath the
highway beside the stream of
gathering.

∎

It is because certain of we are
always driving that the parking lot
matters.

Certain of we are driving to
waking up.

Certain of we are driving back
to clear ideas about what certain
of we are.

Certain of we are driving to
finishing what got interrupted.

Certain of we are driving to
orange, sticky fruit.

Certain of we are driving to the
airplane's heat shimmering off its
wings.

Certain of we are driving to clear
water moving over rocks.

Certain of we are driving to
things are this way, this way.

Certain of we are driving from
what are things.

Certain of we are driving to
waiting.

Certain of we are driving to
thinking in rooms without walls.

Certain of we are driving to
the way of it all being clear.

Certain of we are driving to
bougainvillea.

Certain of we are driving from
little cubicles, overhead lights,
bright flickering screen.

Certain of we are driving from
the way of thinking of it as one to
the way of thinking of it as one
and one.

Certain of we are driving the
metaphor.

．

The metaphor here of how we
need

and how we reach

and certain of us have rights yet
the rights are kept from certain of
us

by certain of us who are owning
place.

Certain of we have rights and
these rights are written so that
there is a possible keeping, a
keeping away, that denies
gathering.

NOVEMBER 30, 2002

Beloveds, we wake up in the morning to darkness and watch it turn into lightness with hope.

Each morning we wait in our bed listening for the parrots and their chattering.

Beloveds, the trees branch over our roof, over our bed, and so realize that when I speak about the parrots I speak about love and their green colors, love and their squawks, love and the discord they bring to the calmness of morning, which is the discord of waking.

When I speak of the parrots I speak of all that we wake to this morning, the Dow slipping yet still ending in a positive mood yesterday, Mission Control, the stalled railcar in space, George Harrison's extra-large will, Hare Krishnas, the city of Man, the city of Danane and the Movement for Justice and Peace and the Ivorian Popular Movement for the Great West, homelessness and failed coups, few leads in the bombing in Kenya.

Today I still speak of the fourteen that are dead in Kenya from earlier in the week, some by their own choice and some by the choices of others, as I speak of the parrots.

And as I speak of the parrots I speak of the day's weather here, the slight breeze and the blanket I pull over myself this morning in the subtropics and then I speak also of East Africa, those detained for questioning, porous borders, the easy availability of fraudulent passports.

I speak of long coastlines and Alexandre Dumas's body covered in blue cloth with the words "all for one, one for all."

I speak of grandsons of black Haitian slaves and what it means to be French.

I speak of global jihad, radical clerics, giant planets, Jupiter, stars' gas and dust, gravitational accretion, fluid dynamics, protoplanetary evolution, the unstoppable global spread of AIDS.

When I speak of the parrots I speak of the pair of pet conures released sometime in 1986 or 1987 that now number at least thirty.

I speak of how they begin their day at sunrise and fly at treetop height southward to rest in the trees near our bed, beloveds, where they rest for about an hour to feed, preen, and socialize before moving on to search for fruits and seeds of wild plum, Christmas berry, papaya, strawberry guava, and other shrubs and trees that were, like them, like us, brought here from somewhere else.

I speak of our morning to come, mundane with the news of it all, with its hour of feeding, preening, and restrained socializing before turning to our separate computers and the wideness of their connections and the probable hourly changes of temperature between 79 and 80 degrees that will happen all day long with winds that begin the day at 12 mph and end it at 8 mph.

When I speak of the green of the parrots I speak of yous and me, beloveds, and our roosts at the bottom of the crater once called Lēʻahi, now called Diamond Head, and I speak of those who encourage us to think of them as roosting with us, Mariah Carey, Jermaine Dupri, Jimmy Jam and Terry Lewis, Jay-Z, Cam'ron, Justin Timberlake, Nick Carter, Rod Stewart, and Shania Twain.

And I speak of the flapping of parrots' wings as they come over the tree that reaches over the bed and the helpless flapping of our wings in our mind, our wings flapping as we are on our backs in our bed at night unable to turn over or away from this, the three-legged stool of political piece, military piece, and development piece, that has entered into our bed at night holding us down sleepless as the parrots have entered into this habitat far away from their origin because someone set them free, someone set them free, and they fly from one place to another, loudly, to remind us of our morning and we welcome this even, stuck on our backs in bed, wings flapping, welcome any diversion from the pieces of the three-legged stool.

NATASHA TRETHEWEY

[B. 1966]

LETTER HOME

New Orleans, November 1910

Four weeks have passed since I left, and still
I must write to you of no work. I've worn down
the soles and walked through the tightness
of my new shoes, calling upon the merchants,
their offices bustling. All the while I kept thinking
my plain English and good writing would secure
for me some modest position. Though I dress each day
in my best, hands covered with the lace gloves
you crocheted—no one needs a *girl*. How flat
the word sounds, and heavy. My purse thins.
I spend foolishly to make an appearance of quiet
industry, to mask the desperation that tightens
my throat. I sit watching—

though I pretend not to notice—the dark maids
ambling by with their white charges. Do I deceive
anyone? Were they to see my hands, brown
as your dear face, they'd know I'm not quite
what I pretend to be. I walk these streets
a white woman, or so I think, until I catch the eyes
of some stranger upon me, and I must lower mine,
a *negress* again. There are enough things here
to remind me who I am. Mules lumbering through
the crowded streets send me into reverie, their footfall

the sound of a pointer and chalk hitting the blackboard
at school, only louder. Then there are women, clicking
their tongues in conversation, carrying their loads
on their heads. Their husky voices, the wash pots
and irons of the laundresses call to me. Here,

I thought not to do the work I once did, back-bending
and domestic; my schooling a gift—even those half days
at picking time, listening to Miss J—. How
I'd come to know words, the recitations I practiced
to sound like her, lilting, my sentences curling up
or trailing off at the ends. I read my books until
I nearly broke their spines, and in the cotton field,
I repeated whole sections I'd learned by heart,
spelling each word in my head to make a picture
I could see, as well as a weight I could feel
in my mouth. So now, even as I write this
and think of you at home, *Good-bye*

is the waving map of your palm, is
a stone on my tongue.

FROM LETTERS FROM STORYVILLE

DECEMBER 1910

Miss Constance Wright
1 Schoolhouse Road
Oakvale, Mississippi

My Dearest Constance,

I am not out-of-doors as you feared,
and though I've had to tuck the blue, wool suit
you gave me, I do now have plenty to eat.
I have no doubt my decision will cause you
much distress, but still I must tell you—
when I had grown too weary to keep up
my inquiries and my rent was coming
due, I had what must be considered
the good fortune to meet Countess P—,
an elegant businesswoman who offered
me a place in her house. I did not accept
then, though I had tea with her—the first
I'd had in days. And later, too hungry
to reason, I spent the last of my purse
on a good meal. It was to her that I went
when I had to leave my hotel, and I am
as yet adjusting to my new life.

This first week I sat — as required —
each evening in the parlor, unnoticed,
the "professor" working the piano
into a frenzy, a single cockroach
scaling the flocked-velvet wallpaper.
The men who've come have called only
on the girls they know — their laughter
trailing off behind them, their gowns
floating past the balustrade. Though
she's said nothing, Countess is indeed
sympathetic. Just the other night
she introduced me to a longtime client
in hopes that he'd take a liking to me.
I was too shy to speak and only pretended
to sip the wine he'd ordered. Of course,
he found me dull and soon excused himself
to find another girl. Part of me was
quite relieved, though I knew I could not
earn a living that way.

                And so, last night
I was auctioned as a newcomer
to the house — as yet untouched, though
Countess knows well the thing from which
I've run. Many of the girls do too,
and some of them even speak of a child
they left behind. The auction was a near
quiet affair — much like the one Whitman

described, the men some wealthy "gentlemen"
from out of town. Countess announced
that I recite poetry, hinting at a more dignified
birth and thus a tragic occasion for my arrival
at her house. She calls me *Violet* now—
a common name here in Storyville—except
that I am the *African Violet* for the promise
of that wild continent hidden beneath
my white skin. At her cue, I walked slowly
across the room, paused in strange postures
until she called out, *Tableau vivant*, and
I could again move—all this to show
the musical undulation of my hips, my grace,
and my patience which was to mean
that it is my nature to please and that I could,
if so desired, pose still as a statue for hours,
a glass or a pair of boots propped upon my back.

And then, in my borrowed gown
I went upstairs with the highest bidder.
He did not know to call me

Ophelia

FROM STORYVILLE DIARY

Bellocq

APRIL 1911

There comes a quiet man now to my room—
Papá Bellocq, his camera on his back.
He wants *nothing*, he says, but to take me
as I would arrange myself, fully clothed—
a brooch at my throat, my white hat angled
just so—*or not*, the smooth map of my flesh
awash in afternoon light. In my room
everything's a prop for his composition—
brass spittoon in the corner, the silver
mirror, brush and comb of my toilette.
I try to pose as I think he would like—shy
at first, then bolder. I'm not so foolish
that I don't know this photograph *we* make
will bear the stamp of his name, not mine.

CHRISTIAN WIMAN

[B. 1966]

CLEARING

It was when I walked lost
in the burn and rust
of late October that I turned
near dusk toward the leaf-screened
light of a green clearing in the trees.
In the untracked and roadless open
I saw an intact but wide open house,
half-standing and half-lost
to unsuffered seasons of wind
and frost: warped tin and broken stone,
old wood combed by the incurious sun.
The broad wall to the stark north,
each caulked chink and the solid hearth
dark with all the unremembered fires
that in the long nights quietly died,
implied a life of bare solitude
and hardship, little to hold
and less to keep, aching days
and welcome sleep in the mind-clearing cold.
And yet the wide sky, the wildflowered ground
and the sound of the wind
in the burn and rust of late October
as the days shortened and the leaves turned
must have been heartening, too,
to one who walked out of the trees
into a green clearing that he knew.

If you could find this place,
or even for one moment feel
in the word-riddled remnants
of what I felt there
the mild but gathering air, see the leaves
that with one good blast would go,
you could believe
that standing in a late weave of light and shade
a man could suddenly want his life,
feel it blaze in him and mean,
as for a moment I believed,
before I walked on.

POŠTOLKA

Prague

When I was learning words
and you were in the bath
there was a flurry of small birds
and in the aftermath

of all that panicked flight,
as if the red dusk willed
a concentration of its light:
a falcon on the sill.

It scanned the orchard's bowers,
then pane by pane it eyed
the stories facing ours
but never looked inside.

I called you in to see.
And when you steamed the room
and naked next to me
stood dripping, as a bloom

of blood formed in your cheek
and slowly seemed to melt,
I could almost speak
the love I almost felt.

Wish for something, you said.
A shiver pricked your spine.
The falcon turned its head
and locked its eyes on mine,

and for a long moment I'm still in
I wished and wished and wished
the moment would not end.
And just like that it vanished.

READING HERODOTUS

Sadness is to lie uneaten
among the buried dead, to die
without feeling a fire
kindled in your honor, that clean smell
of cypress rising and the chants, heat
increasing under you, into you, an old man
whose name the feasters weep and sing.
Confusion is to be born
into a people without names or dreams
to whom the dead must come in the daylight—
brief faces in the clouds, traces of familiar dust
to which you cannot call out, of which you cannot speak
as in the light wind those losses are lost again.
Suddenly, and without sound,
a god comes back, easing into our lives
as if he'd never left, opening
to our opened eyes those carved arms
as if that touch could be a tenderness to us.
Thus a man, a king, who sees a strange tree
burgeoning from the unveiled, inviolate dark
of his own daughter's loins,
wakes in high glee, doom
gathering in his chambers like early light.
So a woman who all night long has prayed
that upon her sons will descend
the greatest blessing that can descend to men,

finds in the first light they will not wake to their names,
their brows cooler than the coolness of dawn.
No telling how she answers this,
if after seeing her sons disposed of
in the custom of that country
—corpses torn by dogs, birds eating out the eyes
to sing from every tree what the dead see—
she curses her gods and desecrates fetishes
or falls to her knees that night breathing
an altogether original language of praise.
No telling if a man might carry
plunder and his own unsevered head
from the man-sized ants no man has seen
to the sweet tombs of a city where the dead rest in honey
always in search of something farther.
Does some dream country come to him at the last
—in the flash of metal, at the height of his own cry—
as to the slaves of certain nomads,
blinded so they will not know their homeland,
the birds one day become familiar,
the earth assumes old scents and contours
and the very air is suddenly sweeter than they can bear.
They are gone now, swirled
in the dark earth with the ones who,
seeing their slaves go mad, killed them,
who are themselves gone, their bones
partaking of the same silence in which lie
all the dog-headed men of the mountains,
headless men with eyes in their chests,

men so immense their shadows were as night,
men carved in marble to whom the gods gave only life enough
to let them fall to their knees . . .
                              Close your eyes
just this side of sleep and you can almost hear them,
all the long wonder of it, the lost gods
and the languages, the strange names and their fates,
lives unlike our own, as alien and unknowable
as the first hour on this earth for a womb-slick babe
around whom the whole tribe has formed a ring,
wailing as one for what the child must learn.

CRAIG ARNOLD

[B. 1967]

HERMIT CRAB

A drifter, or a permanent house-guest,
he scrabbles through the stones, and can even scale
the flaked palm-bark, towing along his latest
lodging, a cast-off periwinkle shell.
Isn't he weighed down? Does his house not pinch?
The sea urchin, a distant relative,
must haul his spiny armor each slow inch
by tooth only—sometimes, it's best to live
nowhere, and yet be anywhere at home.

That's the riddle of his weird housekeeping
—does he remember how he wears each welcome
out in its turn, and turns himself out creeping
unbodied through the sand, grinding and rude,
and does he feel a kind of gratitude?

SCRUBBING MUSSELS

Easy at first to think they're all alike.
But in the time it takes your brush to scour
away the cement their beards secrete to stick
to the rock, to one another, you find the lure

of intimacy a temptation. Palm
cupping each shell, you learn a history
from what you scrape off—limpets, worm-
castings, their own brown crust—the company

they've kept, how many neighbors, on the fringes
or in the thick. This patriarchal shell
suffered a near-mortal crack—hinges
skewed by a scab, its valves will never seal

perfectly, ever. This one lost a chip
of its carapace—the nacre gleams, steel plate
in a war veteran's skull. Here is a coup-
le tangled by their beards—but do they mate?

You can't remember how they reproduce.
Now and then you'll find one open, startle,
fling it aside—your fingers come too close
to what you hoped would stay hidden, the veil

lining the shell, flushed pink, not orange,
no, not yet. Once they are cleaned, and more
or less alike, they're ready to arrange
in the skillet, large enough for a single layer,

with chopped onions and garlic, maybe a pinch
of tarragon—no salt, they will provide
the salt themselves—butter, a half-inch
or so of dry white wine. Replace the lid,

turn on and light the gas. Make sure the match
is thoroughly stubbed out. If you've been tempted
at any point to see in them an image
of yourself, you must make sure your mind is emptied

of all such madness. Mussels cannot mind
the slowly warming pan, the steam, or feel
real pain, which requires sympathy, a kind
of tenderness. The worst, most capable

monsters admit a feeling for the flesh
they brutalize—the inquisitors who cry
with the heretic they rack for a confes-
sion, the kind cop who stops the third degree

to offer coffee, a smoke, the death camp
doctor who celebrates a patient's birthday,
slips him an extra piece of bread—all symp-
athetic men. Think how delicious they

will be, the shells relaxing, giving up their humble
secrets, their self-possession. Your demands
are not so cruel. Don't follow their example.
Slice the lemon. Make sure to wash your hands.

FROM MISTRAL

Speeding across the wide white
slate of the salt flat once   you passed a car
flipped over   you saw the skidmarks
Here the driver took the curve too fast
fishtailed across the shoulder   here he startled
pulled the wheel too hard   spun
suddenly into a blank without horizon
leaving a long scar in the crystal crust

What color car   or who was hurt
are not given for you to know
All you recall are the crates of apples
stacked in the back   that blasted out
of every broken window   spattered
as drops of blood across a snow

HONORÉE FANONNE JEFFERS

[B. 1967]

THE GOSPEL OF BARBECUE

for Alvester James

Long after it was
necessary, Uncle
Vess ate the leavings
off the hog, doused
them with vinegar sauce.
He ate chewy abominations.
Then came high pressure.
Then came the little pills.
Then came the doctor
who stole Vess's second
sight, the predication
of pig's blood every
fourth Sunday.
Then came the stillness
of barn earth, no more
trembling at his step.
Then came the end
of the rib, but before
his eyes clouded,
Uncle Vess wrote
down the gospel
of barbecue.

Chapter one:
Somebody got to die

with something at some
time or another.

Chapter two:
Don't ever trust
white folk to cook
your meat until
it's done to the bone.

Chapter three:
December is the best
time for hog killing.
The meat won't
spoil as quick.
Screams and blood
freeze over before
they hit the air.

Chapter four, Verse one:
Great Grandma Mandy
used to say food
you was whipped
for tasted the best.

Chapter four, Verse two:
Old Master knew to lock
the ham bacon chops
away quick or the slaves
would rob him blind.
He knew a padlock

to the smokehouse
was best to prevent
stealing, but even the
sorriest of slaves would
risk a beating for a full
belly. So Christmas time
he give his nasty
leftovers to the well
behaved. The head ears
snout tail fatback
chitlins feet ribs balls.
He thought gratitude
made a good seasoning.

Chapter five:
Unclean means dirty
means filthy means
underwear worn too
long in summertime heat.
Perfectly good food
can't be no sin.
Maybe the little
bit of meat on ribs
makes for lean eating.
Maybe the pink flesh
is tasteless until you add
onions garlic black
pepper tomatoes
soured apple cider
but survival ain't never been

no crime against nature
or Maker. See, stay alive
in the meantime, laugh
a little harder. Go on
and gnaw that bone clean.

OUTLANDISH BLUES (THE MOVIE)

*... newly arrived Africans were classified in the North American lexicon
as "outlandish" in that they were "strangers to the English language"
and had yet to learn their new roles.* — MICHAEL A. GOMEZ

Where else can you sail across a blue sea
into a horizon emptied of witnesses?
This is the cathartic's truth, the movie mind's eye,
a vibrant ship voyage where the slaves luckily escape,

where the horizon empties of witnesses,
and the food and the water and the mercy run low
on this photogenic voyage where slaves luckily will escape,
but not before sailors throw a few souls in the ocean.

Before the food, water and mercy run low,
watch the celluloid flashes of sexy, tight bodies
that the sailors throw into the mouths of waiting fish,
bodies branded with the Cross, baptized with holy water,

tight-packed bodies flashing across the screen,
Hollywood flat stomachs pressed to buttocks pressed to shoulders
first branded with the Cross, baptized with holy water
and then covered with manufactured filth.

The stomachs press to buttocks press to shoulders
and of course, there is no pleasure in the touch—
under the filth we can see the taut black beauty
and we guiltily consider the following:

Are we sure there was no pleasure in those touches?
Are we sure most kidnapped Africans were not full grown?
We guiltily consider the following:
Were these really children picked for long lives of work?

Are we sure these were not full grown Africans
instead of children stolen or sold from their parents,
picked for long lives of work to be squeezed from them?
Must we think on coins passed between white and black hands?

These were children stolen or sold from their parents
though we don't see any of that on the movie screen.
We don't see coins passed between white and black hands.
We don't see any boys and girls raped by the sailors.

We don't see much of their lives on the screen,
only the clean Bible one of the male slaves is given.
We don't see any boys and girls raped by the sailors,
only prayers for redemption the slave definitely receives.

There are close-ups of the Bible given to a slave
but no questions about the God he sees in his dreams.
Who gives him the redemption I'm sure he receives?
Who will he call on—the God of his parents?

Who is the God he sees in his dreams?
Who placed him in the gut of this three-hour nightmare?
Who will he call on—the God of his parents
or his Bible's Savior, a man who walks on water?

Who placed him in the gut of this three-hour nightmare?
Certainly not the God of cathartic truth
or even the Bible's Savior, a man walking across water,
just right on over blues cast like bait upon the sea.

UNIDENTIFIED FEMALE STUDENT,

FORMER SLAVE

(Talladega College, circa 1885)

You might have heard a story like this one well
but I'm telling this one to you now.
I was five when the soldiers came.

Master worked me twenty years longer.
How could I know? One day he left me alone
and an unwatched pot started to boil. By the time

he came back home I was cleaned of him and singing,
There's a man going round taking names.
Ready, set, and I was gone, walking. Could I see

beyond his yard? Did I have a thought to read or write
or count past God's creation? A barefooted
girl!—and you remember, you woman who will take

your pen to write my life. This is what the truth was like:
Master's clouds followed me to the steps of this school.
Dear reader, when you think on this years after I have died

and I am dust, think on a great and awful morning
when I learned my freedom. Think that the skin on my
back was scared when I dared step out into the world,

when my Master stood trembling and weeping
on his front porch and he cursed me beyond knowing.

DIANE THIEL

(B. 1967)

MEMENTO MORI IN MIDDLE SCHOOL

When I was twelve, I chose Dante's *Inferno*
in gifted class—an oral presentation
with visual aids. My brother, *il miglior fabbro*,

said he would draw the tortures. We used ten
red posterboards. That day, for school, I dressed
in pilgrim black, left earlier to hang them

around the class. The students were impressed.
The teacher, too. She acted quite amused
and peered too long at all the punishments.

We knew by reputation she was cruel.
The class could see a hint of twisted forms
and asked to be allowed to round the room

as I went through my final presentation.
We passed the first one, full of poets cut
out of a special issue of *Horizon*.

The class thought these were such a boring set,
they probably deserved their tedious fates.
They liked the next, though—bodies blown about,

the lovers kept outside the tinfoil gates.
We had a new boy in our class named Paolo
and when I noted Paolo's wind-blown state

and pointed out Francesca, people howled.
I knew that more than one of us not-so-
covertly liked him. It seemed like hours

before we moved on to the gluttons, though,
where they could hold the cool fistfuls of slime
I brought from home. An extra touch. It sold

in canisters at toy stores at the time.
The students recognized the River Styx,
the logo of a favorite band of mine.

We moved downriver to the town of Dis,
which someone loudly re-named Dis and Dat.
And for the looming harpies and the furies,

who shrieked and tore things up, I had clipped out
the shrillest, most deserving teacher's heads
from our school paper, then thought better of it.

At the wood of suicides, we quieted.
Though no one in the room would say a word,
I know we couldn't help but think of Fred.

His name was in the news, though we had heard
he might have just been playing with the gun.
We moved on quickly by that huge, dark bird

and rode the flying monster, Geryon,
to reach the counselors, each wicked face,
again, I had resisted pasting in.

To represent the ice in that last place,
where Satan chewed the traitors' frozen heads,
my mother had insisted that I take

an ice-chest full of popsicles—to end
my gruesome project on a lighter note.
"It *is* a comedy, isn't it," she said.

She hadn't read the poem, or seen our art,
but asked me what had happened to the sweet,
angelic poems I once read and wrote.

The class, though, was delighted by the treat,
and at the last round, they all pushed to choose
their colors quickly, so they wouldn't melt.

The bell rang. Everyone ran out of school,
as always, yelling at the top of their lungs,
The *Inferno* fast forgotten, but their howls

showed off their darkened red and purple tongues.

ECHOLOCATIONS

The waters compassed me about, even to the soul:
the depth closed me round about,
the weeds were wrapped about my head.

—JONAH 2:5

In *Boca Vieja*, on the unsettled stretch of beach
which formed the border between two continents,
a coast where water flowed down from the forest—
I had come to find the furthest distance.
At the end of a labyrinth of fallen boulders,
I came upon the massive skeleton,
the whitened frame reflecting back the sun.
The ribcage formed a passage to the sea,
where thin rivers ran between the bones,
dividing further as they reached the ocean.
The skull, half-buried in the sand, resembled
a house from some forgotten fairy tale.
I climbed in through the porthole of an eye,
looked out the double circles filled with light.

I found my way down what was once her throat
and wandered through the gallery of bones.
Her ribcage framed the sea, the sky, the trees—
each canvas a vast range of blues and greens.
I reached the place that must have held her heart,

knowing, as a child, I could have fit inside
her vessels, even. I could have hidden there.
The tide was coming in, reclaiming things
clinging to the curved bones or roaming the shore—
the tiny hydroid forests with their medusae,
the limpets like small traveling volcanoes,
the scrolled whelks, drawing their maze of whorls,
only to be washed away. This was the end
of the whale's road. She passed her life to thousands.

I felt the sun-warm bone against my skin—
and a sudden heartbeat in the skeleton.
Her heart beat with a distant beckoning,
and in a moment I was with her, traveling
the *hwaelweg*, the road itself another kenning.
The ocean set the cadence, the swells singing
a line, receiving back another line—
in each reply, the slightest variation.
Our languages returning to the sounds
encoded in our strands, the spiral towers
of our helixes spinning round each other.
The calls reverberating through the waters
to navigate the depths, to guide us through
one ocean to another, the dark indigos,

the song returning from the deepest blues.

IPHIGENEIA (SAPPHICS FROM TAURIS)

Song has come tonight to allow my questions.
How did I arrive on this unknown ocean?
Life passed in the fall of that long blade, only
following orders.

Sacrificed for "favorable winds" but somehow
plucked from Charon just when I tasted iron.
Someone took my place. I could feel the bones and
flesh fill the space left.

Blood in my eyes, I could feel fur and skin wrap
round me, hear the voice that was not my own, scream
out—in language all of us understand, yet
let it be uttered.

If we survive, memory makes one part split
from the other. One of me died that evening.
One of me seems safe, but will always carry
Fear like a stone child.

Now, with wine-dark hands, I am made to carry
out the very act which my scars remember.
How can I allow yet another brother
such final terror.

BHANU KAPIL

[B. 1968]

FROM *THE VERTICAL INTERROGATION*

OF STRANGERS

28. WHERE DID YOU COME FROM / HOW DID YOU ARRIVE?

I don't know how this corresponds to the world: I miss his letters arriving, holding them between my fingertips like stems: the minutes before I open them, regardless of this morning, of never again being able to . . .

Sometimes you may never see your home again. An ache in the lower back, the methodical preparation of basil soup, the sweetness of the juice of the broken stems. I cover my face with my hands. Breathe in. When the violet colour comes, I leave my house, without shoes. This hour's so hungry. (The last things—the silk of his shirt, my forehead pressed to his chest, when I could not look at him, the glass or bone or threshold of his chest—are the ones I keep.)

I think of my mother, as a bride, leaving India. The softness of the tip of her nose, her brow, breasts, red palms pressed to the glass: she is staring at the tar steaming after rain. (The black water of her eyes falling in lines.)

48. WHAT ARE THE CONSEQUENCES OF SILENCE?

There are three kinds of hunger:

1. I dreamed I gave birth to slab after slab of fresh meat, and that my mother held my feet down with her hands. When I woke up, I had an intense longing for the lentil soup my mother used to make, when I was sick, and home from school. Lots of lemon. Bay leaves. A spoonful of brown sugar. Something sweet and tangy at the same time.

2. He is kissing your feet, your knees, your thighs. You reach down and pull him up to your mouth by his hair. This is a specific example of a hunger that is immigrant, in that you find yourself unable to ask for what you really want.

3. The hunger that's made of eggshells: the most unstable version of the colour white. You are wearing chiffon. A sari made of magnolia petals. Your innards throb. For whatever reason, you will never see this person again. It is ten years from now. You wake up at four a.m., on the verge of panic.

72. WHAT ARE THE CONSEQUENCES OF SILENCE?

I am not writing about myself as a rational human being. I am writing about the substances of an animal and female life: magic, pain, the cracked nails of four feet, and the days like this one, when it is difficult to speak to a good-looking man. He returns with sesame seeds, unleavened bread, ginger and coriander powders, coffee, olives, chocolate, yoghurt, onions, cucumbers, potatoes, and a quart of milk. He thinks I am a woman because he bathes me, puts his hands on the sides of my face, tells me I am beautiful. Yes. Okay. But there is something hard between my lungs. It is the size of a blood-orange from northern California.

97. WHO IS RESPONSIBLE FOR THE SUFFERING OF YOUR MOTHER?

When my mother's uncle was dying, I went to his house to say good-bye. I was twenty years old. When he saw my face, he started crying. My mother said it was because I looked so much like his sister, Shanta, who had died when she was nineteen. She bled to death when she climbed the mountain behind her house. My mother said she should never have gone for a walk when she had her menses. I knew immediately, I don't know how, that she had died, hæmorrhaging, during a miscarriage. That she had climbed the mountain on purpose. But nobody would ever say that.

(Shame may be fatal)

DAVID KEPLINGER

[B. 1968]

THE DISTANCE BETWEEN ZERO AND ONE

In April the carnival came.
The ice and the factory lot,
the carnival rides huffing black stripes of smoke. . . .

Pig slaughter music.
My great love stirring the blood with her hands.
Others cleaning the long blue
intestines in snowdrifts
filled with tiny stones.

TOWARDS A RECONCILIATION

WITH DISORDER

Nothing can be described. In this
The work of art is mere forgiveness.
I knew a man whose life was irreconcilable.
We must look into the sun, he said. Let's say
The gesture of compassion is an attack
Against form, against structure, dubious
Shell in which we trust. This man was crass,
Nearly to the point of clarity. He showed me how
He fixed his mouth over a boy soldier's wound,

To save the soldier from bleeding to death.
What's one sun colliding with the others?
What's one death if it can't be everything? Anyway,
The soldier died. Forgive me, this man said.

BASIC TRAINING

His sits on the Greyhound bus.
Just below his window
Where the driver smokes,
The year is 1955.

He's on his way to basic training.
The father sells insurance
And has been on strike
And has time

To take his son to the station.
He has time
To make a little
Chit chat. He talks about

Some money he has earned
Selling rare coins.
He talks to his son
From the street.

The passing traffic
Shakes the Greyhound bus.
The father lights a cigarette
And gazes towards

Some small, indefinable point
On the horizon.
The son looks at it, too.
They look at it and look at it.

The son would like a cigarette.
He would like his father
To tell him what he sees.
But the father says

One more thing:
What was it? The other
Will always have to wonder,
Have to tell about,

Like this,
As the bus shoves off;
And the door closes;
The enormous wing.

A. E. STALLINGS

[B. 1968]

AFTERSHOCKS

We are not in the same place after all.
The only evidence of the disaster,
Mapping out across the bedroom wall,
Tiny cracks still fissuring the plaster—
A new cartography for us to master,
In whose legend we read where we are bound:
Terra infirma, a stranger land, and vaster.
Or have we always stood on shaky ground?
The moment keeps on happening: a sound.
The floor beneath us swings, a pendulum
That clocks the heart, the heart so tightly wound,
We fall mute, as when two lovers come
To the brink of the apology, and halt,
Each standing on the wrong side of the fault.

SINE QUA NON

Your absence, father, is nothing. It is nought—
The factor by which nothing will multiply,
The gap of a dropped stitch, the needle's eye
Weeping its black thread. It is the spot
Blindly spreading behind the looking glass.
It is the startled silences that come

When the refrigerator stops its hum,
And crickets pause to let the winter pass.

Your absence, father, is nothing—for it is
Omega's long last O, memory's elision,
The fraction of impossible division,
The element I move through, emptiness,
The void stars hang in, the interstice of lace,
The zero that still holds the sum in place.

FIRST LOVE: A QUIZ

He came up to me:

    A. in his souped-up Camaro

    B. to talk to my skinny best friend

    C. and bumped my glass of wine so I wore the ferrous stain on my
       sleeve

    D. from the ground, in a lead chariot drawn by a team of stallions
       black as crude oil and breathing sulfur; at his heart, he sported
       a tiny golden arrow

He offered me:

    A. a ride

    B. dinner and a movie, with a wink at the cliché

    C. an excuse not to go back alone to the apartment with its sink
       of dirty knives

D. a narcissus with a hundred dazzling petals that breathed a
   sweetness as cloying as decay

I went with him because:
   A. even his friends told me to beware
   B. I had nothing to lose except my virginity
   C. he placed his hand in the small of my back and I felt the tread
      of honeybees
   D. he was my uncle, the one who lived in the half-finished
      basement, and he took me by the hair

The place he took me to:
   A. was dark as my shut eyes
   B. and where I ate bitter seed and became ripe
   C. and from which my mother would never take me wholly back,
      though she wept and walked the earth and made the bearded
      ears of barley wither on their stalks and the blasted flowers
      drop from their sepals
   D. is called by some men hell and others love
   E. all of the above

JENNY FACTOR

[B. 1969]

SONNET

There were lies. You knew, but then forgot
the child peeking around the corner, hiding
from you. Wind sifts through the beechnut
arbor. Peripheral, the real story goes trailing
moonlike, behind the car window, just beyond
view. And how bad is it to have believed the best
of your story, or a lover's; to have rested
in that sweetness that is sweetest
when forgot: a dog's head on your lap, fuchsia blooming
in a pot, whether tended to or not? Now the child
in the closet wonders (frightened, cold)
if the darkness will lift before dinner. *Hold
out your hands, Mother,* he thinks, hoping.
The door swings open. The face is wild.

RIQUEZA

*Tengo la dicha fiel / y la dicha perdida:
la una coma rosa, / la otra coma espina . . .*
—GABRIELA MISTRAL

Although the Eaton Wash was pink with ghost
and dust, I took the horsy path again
down to where the water and the rain

meet. My toes are happiest when placed
where specks of guppies cluster light and tumble
water on my skin up to my ankles.
Moss in brackish eddy rides the ripples.
Sparrows dart away from me like troubles.
Sagey, dusty, doggy smell of trail
drags my body back to what is real:
I have a faithful joy and a joy that is lost.

The night you flew twenty hours home from Oman, got
Sam to sleep, we sat on the kitchen floor,
blasted with a clear domestic light,
and I told you I couldn't stay married anymore.
We took our regal bands from our ring fingers
but yours wouldn't budge—knuckles outsized joints.
Was the Divine Jester making points?
Perhaps. We ended at the sink—in blood, cold water,
I holding your whole body from behind.
Although it didn't imply change, it implied,
I have been faithful, Joy. I have been lost.

Mommy, can't we have "old family" back?
I want you and my dad to live together.
Is Grandpa Andy really Daddy's father?
Are *hot* and *cold* or *east* and *beast* a match?
Why can't I make the video in my head
play only good dreams? Mommy, don't help.
Mom, you're the best mom in the whole world!
Look, I poured the milk out by myself.

Do you miss me when I'm at my dad's?
How come you have my helmet but not my knee pads?
I have a faithful joy and a joy that is lost.

Eaton Wash. I walked there with my love.
Eaton Wash. I dreamed there of another.
One who'd gnaw my insides like a bone.
One who'd tease my tears out like a mother.
One I wanted till my nipples milked.
Dusk spinning with life inside her room,
cranky, cunning, keen insightful talk
in that garden overrun with bloom.
Moments would expand there like a lung.
Raw, uncertain, realizing, unstrung,
I am unfaithful, Joy, but far from lost.

Echo the perfect conquest of the sea
over every groomed, tamed, patient shore.
Stitch a salvaged piece of what I've torn
into the quilt my son keeps on his knee.
Rich with purple martins, rich with sparrow,
live oak, flat bush, goldfinch, tufted brown
stream birds that dart off from me close to ground.
I am as rich with purple as with sorrow.
Thirty-one, an acorn, dropped, reborn,
resting on the dust (or stone) exhaust.
Oh how loved is the rose, how loving the thorn!
I have a faithful joy and a joy that is lost.

SCOTCH AND SODA

The front door slipped from its latch and he
came in—the man you're married to and love.
He knows about this "us," this you-and-me,
and it is for his sake that words like "love"
and "tomorrow" don't flow between us easily;
when Ella slips into the groove on the CD
player, your shirt lifts above your head
(my ice settling in my glass, I feel sour beads
of sweat from the summer heat rising
on my skin). Here the truth is surprising
even to me: I don't mind what we *don't*
say, what you *can't* feel. "I love you" is scary.
I mean something lighter. What I want:
Lay with me, wide-eyed, wary.

KEVIN PRUFER

[B. 1969]

STRANGE WOOD

When they looked at their boy
they thought, this is strange wood
growing among us.

When I opened my eyes,
he said earlier. When I opened my eyes
she was there.

Down the street, older boys
dig their bear traps, hide
their forts among thick brambles.

The sun (the glowing
face of his clock)
slips behind the oak trees.

Where are you where are you,
he thinks from his bed,
and the cat is there again.

She is a spring.
She stretches, uncoiling,
rolls onto her side on the bed.

Downstairs, his parents say:
He is old enough, he can know
about loss. He is old enough.

I haven't been gone, the cat whispers.
I have been in the yard
with the lightning bugs.

He touches her fur, soft as grass.
She tells him all the roads
go to the same place.

His parents are talking
about the things he does not need.
Coddling, the mother says.

The clock, the golden sun,
hums sweetly and he
closes his eyes.

The cat, lazy as a pillow,
purrs all the things
they'll never tell him.

ON FINDING A SWASTIKA CARVED ON A TREE IN THE HILLS ABOVE HEIDELBERG

Later, on the Neckar's oil-slick banks,
I fed a two-headed swan a stale bread crust.
The healthy head ate;
the other, featherless, eyes closed or undeveloped,

dragged from the end of its garden-hose neck
in the mud on the shore.

Meanwhile, all along Schwartz Strasse,
as they do every day, the citizens sat
in pairs at their outdoor cafe tables
swallowing schnitzel, sighing at the sun's descent.
They shredded their napkins
then rubbed the rims of their wine glasses
until the evening was filled
with a crystal air-raid siren sound.

The night floated down like a thousand allies
lashed to black parachutes.

LOVE POEM

It was water, hardened
into stones; it was sky, fallen
in rocky chunks. No, you said, it's just
the runoff from a hundred-years defunct
iron furnace around the bend, the extra stuff
that boiled to the top then cooled.
The river washed it to us in pieces,
swirls of blue on blue—blues
of every kind. I took a few,
anyway, lined them on the shelf above our bed.

DONNA STONECIPHER

[B. 1969]

THE NEEDLE'S EYE

In the letter I want to write but won't I'd tell him this: It is easier for the camel to squeeze through the needle's eye than for the watchful to enter the beautiful kingdom. If I daydream about living in a convent for a time, it doesn't mean I don't fear the silence that renders everything black and white. In the courtyard a drill clatters; the mirrors inside the birds' chests reflect this dark noise until their own throats open. If he wanted me on my knees so I wanted him; and so we were doubly unleveraged. This is the city, there is nothing to take us out of ourselves. Things are surprisingly tolerable until I touch my own body: It knows my hand is not his, it wants to murder me for this.

THE CHASE

Does the snake-charmer truly charm the snake, or is it the idea of the snake that charms the charmer into configuring the flute, the lips, the spell, in the first place? This notion of desire as reciprocal gives the lie

to such satires as unrequited love. Last night the birds did *not* suspend their joyful bickering while the woman cried for help in the park at 4 a.m. Row upon row of darkened windows, like sealed mouths,

kept to themselves. The one window with a light on was a face wet
with innocence, the gift some of us wish to spend more hurriedly than
others, as though it were a miasma precluding pure vision, who can say

at precisely what moment the masks make the costume ball begin.
In the second grade I outran Reza Khan from one end of the green
playground to the other, watching the grass lilt up under my feet; I out-
ran his little lips

that wanted to kiss me, or some other girl, it was the chase that mat-
tered, in the historical moment, in the springtime, in a foreign coun-
try, in the late 1970s. In the back seat of rented cars I was gluttonous

with my daydreams like American bubblegum, a whole pack to my-
self, using this or that girl I had seen in the airport, at the hotel pool,
whose sequined swimsuit and back-flip I wished were mine, and whose
life

I then appropriated, as though it were me remote in sequins,
clutched tight as a fist in a back-flip, this was all long before sex, a glim-
mer in my eye, ascended. For a time it was the rage to hold your arms
so tight

around a girl you made her faint, the boys wanted it too, I saw the
stairs back home like a ghostly ladder to an unsought answer, then
came to under a circle of boys with my T-shirt pushed above my

tiny breasts. It happened in the hotel garden. My cupboards were
bare. Before we even knew what rape was we wanted to accuse our P.E.
teacher of it, that fascist, though in fact we had no idea

what that meant, either. I am one of these who has no use for knowledge until its impassable bulk blocks my path, for instance, why was Deedee Sadigh, a better runner than me, back there in a heap on the grass, being covered with kisses

by Reza Khan? Was that his name? I remember hers better, as I remember all the girls unruly like vetch and helleborine flowering in the plot of my girlhood, tyrannical virgin queens, while the boys are almost all

vague—pale shavings of bark. There were enough pistils and stamens then that we did not notice the trees. In fact my heart was broken by a girl, this was many years before a man said to me, in college,

half of desire is awareness of the other's desire, which made my nightly sessions at the mirror downright erotic. If anyone had told me I had need of sequined swimsuits, filched inventories, I would have said no, I was sovereign

of my own demesne. But why were satin pillows the scene of so many girls' nightly dreams of transgression? The rapist and the ravisher each held out hands stigmataed with sticky candy, and any good girl

knew to back away from both. In truth in class we read so many books about rape and war and rape in war that at night I began to bandage my own body, as though the wounds had opened their manifold

red mouths all over me. What, after all, was "repudiation of the masculine" but a wish to remember the heroine? There was a familiar ring to charming and spurning, running and running, a resurrected belief that it was she who could not be caught who would be ever sought, something I read in a book somewhere, how wearying it is to pick up the receiver and dial when you know for certain

the dialee will answer. The logic in Daphne's feathery tree. When did we learn that exaggerated rejection is a garden-marker for buried desire? And still I let the phone ring, though I am home, I have been

found. But last night there was a woman crying for help in the park, I went down to look but was too afraid to look deeper, to sacrifice my looking at the black altar of the bushes, why is the line so fine between ravishment

and horror, the mind of the woman couldn't tell you, it is in a faint, and why will my legs not run, as in the old dream, though he is in pursuit? And suddenly he blocks my path, he is impassable, and I sink into a heap

on the grass, where he whispers in my ear about his great-grandmother's village, at the end of the war, and how, when the Russians came to liberate this village, all the men were still away, and so the soldiers

raped the women, well I mean (he said), the women wanted it, when the soldiers came knocking, the women opened up their doors, they hitched up their skirts, the women—let the soldiers—in

THE FORTUNE

It is a place for which some have spent their lives sighing, a place of burnt-sugar plains and golden weight. Note how the flowers are untroubled. Though secrets are buried all around them in the dirt, their petals are white and not off-white.

As to what is revealed—the sky with its great loaves and fishes alludes a little. "To believe in happiness," the fortune said, "is to worship at the altar of unhappiness." Other sagesse waits, enthroned on your shelves, with grand indifference for your hand.

When the flashlight has illuminated every hiding-place in the house, the insomniac may sleep, dowsing suspicions like sparks one by one. Then the camera pans from the contented face of the sleeper to the earring lying at an unnatural angle on the stair.

What if you could set aside a bit of what might save you for when the coming abundance dies—oh, as it does—on the vine? Just a minute ago there were vistas, seascapes, bellevues, panoramas—now your one small room and its swags.

One summer I saw a girl sunbathing like a grave in a bed of obstreperous weeds. I have seen grown men and women nestle down into filthy sheets. The map was torn right where the little starred destination should have been.

The fortune said, "It's not that the world keeps secrets from you, but that you let yourself be crushed by its secrets." The policeman turned the corner. Some lighthouses are not benevolent, but halo each egress with incriminating white.

See sympathy, the tugboat? Its captain keeps no log for the notes of the beloved, who is plotting his own course all the while. And, incandescent with the light of their misapprehension, the lovers are tugged through the dark to open sea.

MORRI CREECH

[B. 1970]

FIELD KNOWLEDGE

for Kevin Meaux

KITFIELD, S.C.

As if time were a pearl of great price still treasured up here
among snags of sumac, dockweed and the froth of honeysuckle,
fallows so cluttered with scrub pine a backhoe would slip its gear,

as if you could prize from weeds and loam one immaculate
hour, one orient pearl buried at the damp root, and lift it clear
of the years of corn stalks, furrows, hay rakes freckled with scat—.

It was late summer in the year. Wind worried the pine limbs,
shifted the scattered grain in the clawfoot tub where the horses ate.
There was no following the sound of that wind back to the hymns

the Huguenot fathers sang here. No stone or fence rail
marked where the chapel was that men stripped to the bare frames
nor marked where the plundered brick foundation lay, the bell

hauled off, stolen or bartered, and melted for pig iron in 1864,
the quoins and brass fixtures ferried upriver for quick sale,
all the old bricks new-laid for the grade school and general store.

To find that place again you'd need more than the cicada's shell
jeweling the oak, the daubers' mortared nest, need more
than the slurred scripture the snake traces on the floor of the stable.

You'd have to pray and wait like a prophet for adequate vision,
for those days torn from the calendars to rise and reassemble
page by page, have to wait for the oak to climb back into the acorn,

pray until the names for the field wandered back to their source,
the long skein of syllables unwinding through the successions,
Kitfield, Keats Field, Keith's Field, the river reversing its course,

the flame leaping into the matchhead, the oil-soaked wick unlit
again, that set the Huguenot church ablaze, and the hoarse
winds of the hurricane hushed to a held breath in the starlight.

Granted that vision, what might you hope to find here? —
the standing chapel, after the worst wind lashed its spire in 1838
and the steeple passed safe through the storm's eye? But fire

spilled from the lantern where John Keith lay drunk in the vestry,
flames rose despite the rain-swept wind and flooded river,
and all of it—chapel, flame, John Keith—slipped clear of history,

leaving behind a ten-acre tract of dockweed and dried marl,
the still-winged choirs of mockingbirds perched in their hickory
pews, and a story nothing redeems, neither chapel nor pearl.

■

Hard to distinguish memory's embellishments from the prose
of fields, to untangle those prodigal tales wrought at the set table
from the plain-stitched phrasings of bramble and mallow rose.

But, next to Christ's wine at Cana, Noah's dove, and the hot coal
held to the prophet's lips, it all seemed clear enough, that blaze
kindling in my grandmother's talk over purlieu rice and fried quail,

the chapel razed down to charred bricks before the coffee
cooled in her cup and the gravy congealed in its chipped bowl,
so that I knew she had it right, each storm gust and pine tree

fixed in its place, sure as Shadrach's furnace, Nebuchadnezzar,
Eden, or the burning bush. Strange, then, to hear that same story
turned apocryphal in the mouths of uncles and cousins, to hear

the storm winds blown a full month clear of the chapel flames,
the weather so calm that August night not the least leaf or briar
stirred, nor the least bead of rain troubled the window frames,

and those storied bricks, broadcast like fragments of the True Cross
gone, that some claimed lay mortared in a hundred homes,
the church built not from masonwork but heart pine and cypress,

until each detail seemed swept back to that vault of speculation
and possibility where the snowflake is conceived, storehouse
where the hours are forged and kept, where brick and hurricane

alike are kilned or whirled to certainties. What's left but the rage
to believe the past is true, *know* it happened, to believe in blown rain
and chapel ashes, in John Keith who named this fallow acreage

of dockweed when he lay drunk and burning or, sober
as starlight, stuffed the doorjambs and window seams with pages
torn from a dozen bibles, then tossed an oil lamp to light the fire

blazing beyond memory or years?
                              That fire still draws me to the field
where, year after year, neighbors and near relations all swear
It happened yonder, point to where they're sure the lantern spilled,

where those flames still seethe up from the pale roots of sumac
to the first red autumn leaves, and blackberry brambles yield
a fruit sweet as the nectared pulp of sugar cane, growing in black

clusters, big as walnuts, blackberries they swear will boil
down to an ambrosial jam that, kept too long, turns thick
and bitter on the shelf, sharp as a taste of tallow and lamp oil.

ENGINE WORK: VARIATIONS

June morning. Sunlight flashes though the pines.
Blue jays razz and bicker, perch on a fence post
back of my grandfather's yard. His stripped engines
clutter the lawn. And everywhere the taste
of scuppernongs just moments off the vines,
so sour that you would swear the mind has traced
a pathway through the thicket, swear the past
comes clear again, picked piecemeal from the dust—.

■

Or else it's late — September — and the shade
thicker than I recall: those cardinals,
finches or mockingbirds still haven't made
a sound all afternoon, though ripe fruit swells
on vine, or branch — or bramble. Thus the frayed
edge of recollection slowly ravels
away to nothing, until that place is gone
where the heart would know its object, and be known.

■

All right. Not to begin with those backlit pines,
those scuppernongs, the jay perched on a branch
of sweet gum — no, oak, I think. With what, then?
With my grandfather holding a torque wrench
or ratchet? Some old engine's stammer and whine
before it starts, or doesn't — a house finch,
singing or silent? Language, too, seems wrong,
though it's all I have. *Grandfather. Scuppernong.*

■

To fix him in some moment, word for word,
that man who taught me gears and cylinders, sweat,
precision of machinery — the hard
love of assembling things.
                                      I know the heat
all summer hung like a scrim where pistons fired
and the boy I was watched in the raw sunlight.

Spilled oil rainbowed in its shallow pan.
One birdcall, maybe; fruit on a trellised vine . . .

■

Impossible not to change things, move the words
from here to there. It's late now. Nothing's settled—
not engine noise or the sound of one far bird
the mind sings true. Which version of the world
should I believe? This morning in the yard
scuppernongs hang and sweeten. Pine boughs yield
some fragment of the blue jay's call, a sound
the resonant air repeats but cannot mend.

GLEANINGS

for Hattie

To see them for what they are, not to make
more of them than the afternoon allows:
starlings among the sweet gum limbs, a rake
propped beneath those leaves the wind will take,
my child gathering feathers beside the house—
a sleight of season, when some moment scatters
its riches across the lawn. Nothing to do
with dates or futures and, I'd guess, small matter
in the year's turning.

But I remember, too,
a thousand starlings in my father's yard,
his Chevy in the drive, a smell of leaves
clear as the feather in my daughter's hand—
a swatch of consequence the mind weaves
from history and chance, so that it's hard,
watching it all, not to construe some meaning
from starling, rake, limb, leaf, the child who stands
gathering feathers beneath the shade of wings.

DEVIN JOHNSTON

[B. 1970]

FACES

I.

What compulsion brought me here
inching toward
an atmosphere so rarefied
as to be unbreathable?

The bulk of time was spent
in the extreme
squalor of a high camp, and then
suddenly we started after

bird-like crampon tracks
past séracs, unstable towers—
and up a face on which
no water fell, and nothing grew.

All substance would persist
in its own mode.
At the moraine's upper end
a bergschrund gaped between

granite and calving glacier,
calling on reserves
of concentration.
An infant's features

glowed beneath
the frangible rime;
taking off one glove,
I plunged my hand

into the snow.
Clearing clotted ice
from my oxygen mask,
I found myself seated,

and Fischer gone—
alerted to
the unreliability
of mind at high altitude.

II.

There comes, just before
blacking out,

a moment
of sweetness and levity—

irony without egress,
the tenor of our times.

White-out
above day's face—

inching slow
toward empty space.

LOS ANGELES

The Colorado River flows—
sans silt—through fluted taps
in Universal City. Saturn nears.

Beneath millennia and shale
a riot growth of giant fern
and brontosauri decompose—
but through the auspices
of wildcats, blaze
                    in incandescent beads
along a sliding mirror: long extinct,
their ghosts reticulate the hills
and hulks of studios—an Oz
of local urgencies.

Beneath the moon, emotions are
but vectors, dragging
                    distant objects near.

As daikon sputters on an open flame,
the owner of Pagoda Inn
cradles the phone against
his shoulder. Neither party speaks,
yet leagues of fiber-optic lines
exchange their silences.

THE LIFE OF WOOD

The name is Wood,
though some would say
I'm living flesh.
You see this scar

across my thumb?
I took a saw
to prune some shrubs
while sucking down

another beer
and never felt
it catch and kick—
but saw the blood.

When we were small
my sister flung
a spitting pan
against my ribs,

which left this pale
and waxy patch
(for weeks I lay
alone in bed).

I am without
profession, but
not quite so dumb
as flames infer:

xyloid, that's
a word which means
the same as wood.
I've tried to graft

another life
to mine and make
the juncture smooth.
But scars outlast

both consciouness
and cause—old facts
initialed in
a valentine,

Atlanta, rings
of time within
electric bulbs;
The Life of Wood.

I lean against
a rake and watch
two contrails cross,
then blow apart;

as I once could—
before I had
to harden from
the center out.

PAISLEY REKDAL

[B. 1970]

A CRASH OF RHINOS

What's your pet name? Collective noun?
What will Snookums do today? Your bedmate
pulls quarters magically from behind your ear, one
for each hour you've spent together. When he stops
there's fifty cents sliding into the sheets and his tongue
covering the pink cauliflower of your nipple. "Beautiful
defects," he whispers into your body. "Ah, Nature." Roll away,
don't care when he calls you "Thumper." By noon you'll be
nose to nose anyway, a sloth of bears, snoozing
your way into this relationship.

Ah, Nature. You could tell him its startling fact
is not its defects but its sameness. A uniformity
suggestive of some single-cell prototype, our Adam/Eve
genome plucked, as scientists think, from the thread
of a lightning bolt. Darling, today you're more
than anonymous, one sexy blip among the thousand
couples grunting in each other's arms; defined by Loving,
your action. Flying geese only recognized
by the form they make in the sky.
A crash of rhinos, piece of asses. Stinkhead:
everything comes in boring droves of hogs.

This is how you got here. Mid-morning he tallies your union
in terms of snakes, tarantulas, the evolutionary needs
of common flagellates till you scorn science: its primal

urge to pair like sacred cows shoved ass to ass in circles
for defense. A clutch of penises! What is love but fear?
That soft storm at your periphery, sudden hand
pushing you below surface? Thoughts, as you age or sicken,
sifted from consciousness like dusts of starlings: Love me,
little lamb. No one should die alone.

Sweetheart, all your friends are married.
Packs of teazles? Kerfs of panters? A multiplicity of spouses.
Today only two quarters protect you
from loneliness. It's out of your hands. The job
didn't pan, checks bounce, 2 a.m. is its own
worst child. This is your last magic trick.
"Kumquat," he whispers. Lover. Loved one.
And the soul begs always, *Leave me leave me*
while the body says simply, *Stay.*

SIX GIRLS WITHOUT PANTS

There is enough to warn us. Like this one

in the waiting room with its drapes pinned
as two blue lids. Her head is stapled
and all the fingers crushed,
the nails like drupelets in a blackberry.

I work with those arriving first,
fleshing out forms
with inked-in detail: which muscles look slackened, broke
in the lime-colored light; just evidence
enough to indicate love

was this woman's mortal sport and safety

merely skimmed the surface.
Like the time five girlfriends and I drove
into Tennessee to look for waterfalls
and came upon the Klansmen rattling change
for library funds in coffee cans instead.
Around them? Tender grasses, fields
blushing with wildflowers in red and yellow.

There is nothing to be afraid of

if it is only anecdote.
Not here, where the wild, unnatural
smoke from mufflers wafted through open windows
around our six throats; the waiting, the danger
cloaked in pristine sheets sweet lovers
might once have tumbled in.

Not at the falls where we fought

through water so insistent
the rush gagged our opened mouths
as we swam to the wet tree notched

in granite to our right.

We were merely six girls struggling
toward the surface
when our toes touched something sharp.

We'd tucked earrings, keys, credit cards in shoes,
left our pants on the shore so water wouldn't
suck us down. We'd drive back

in wet t-shirts and underwear to dry,
our thighs dipped in sunlight
on the car seats. High up in the truck,
no one could look down at us
and see. We joked

about this nakedness
all the way back to the city. This invisible,
this ridiculous,

vulnerability.

STRAWBERRY

I am going to fail.
I'm going to fail cartilage and plastic, camera and arrow.
I'm going to fail binoculars and conjugations,

all the accompanying musics: *I am failing,*
I must fail, I can fail, I have failed
the way some women throw themselves
into lovers' arms or out trains,
fingers crossed and skirts billowing
behind them. I'm going to fail
the way strawberry plants fail,
have dug down hard to fail, shooting
brown runners out into silt, into dry gray beds,
into tissue and rock. I'm going to fail
the way their several hundred hearts below surface
have failed, thick, soft stumps desiccating
to tumors; the way roots wizen in the cold
and cloud black, knotty as spark plugs, cystic
synapses. I'm going to fail light and stars and tears.
I'm going to fail the way cowards only wish they could fail,
the way the brave refuse to fail or the vain fear to,
believing that to stray even once from perfection
is to be permanently cast out, Wandering Jew
of failure, Adam of failure, Sita of failure; that's the way
I'm going to fail, bud and creosote and cloud.
I'm failing pet and parent. I'm failing the food
in strangers' stomachs, the slender inchoate rings
of distant planets. I'm going to fail these words
and the next and the next. I'm going to fail them,
I'm going to fail her—trust me, I've already failed him—
and the possibility of a *we* is going to sink me
like a bad boat. I'm going to fail the way
this strawberry plant has failed, alive without bud,
without fruit, without tenderness, hugging itself

to privation and ridiculous want.
I'm going to fail simply by standing in front of you,
waving my arms in your face as if hailing a taxi:
I'm here, I'm here, please don't forget me,
though you already have, I smell it, even cloaked
with soil, sending out my slender fingers for you,
sending out all my hair and tongue and brain.
I'm going to fail you just as you're going to fail me,
urging yourself further down to sediment
and the tiny, trickling filaments of damp;
thirsty, thirsty, desperate to drown
if even for a little while, if even for once:
to succumb, to be destroyed,
to die completely, to fail the way I've failed
in every particular sense of myself,
in every new and beautiful light.

MARY SZYBIST

[B. 1970]

FIRST CONFESSION

So I bound the devil in chains and beat him.
Oh, he was sore. He admitted his poor
tactics. "Lady, have pity—on me—"
he begged, but I wagged my dogs on.

Or rather one dog. My sorry mutt
whose damp black nose nudged deep
into the demon's thigh. I raised his leg
and flopped it toward the dog who raised

her lips to growl. The devil tried to play
dead. He stared ahead, his one eye in,
the other hanging by its one black thread.
I wound my fingers round that strand, held down

his soft black head and yanked. Why should I pity
him—limp, one-eyed, and neckless?
Even the dog lost interest, plodding
to the window where the sugary snow

fell into the sloping branches
of a poplar. Or rather lots of poplars—
they went past where I could see—
the deepening, unbroken white stretched far

past me. I sat back, decided I
would watch the window as a picture
nailed there, fast. The frame hung still. The snow
blew back and forth and then it stopped.

The picture became just what I thought a picture
should: single slice of branch against a cloud.
No creep, no heave, nothing but reach
cut clean and clear into hereafter.

VIA NEGATIVA

Sometimes it's too hard with words or dark or silence.
Tonight I want a prayer of high-rouged cheekbones
and light: a litany of back-lit figures,
lithe and slim, draped in fabrics soft and wrinkleless and pale
as onion slivers. Figures that won't stumble or cough:
sleek kid-gloved Astaires who'll lift
ladies with glamorous sweeps in their hair—
They'll bubble and glitter like champagne.
They'll whisper and lean and waltz and wink effortlessly
as figurines twirling in music boxes, as skaters in their dreams.

And the prayer will not be crowded.
You'll hear each click of staccato heel
echo through the glassy ballrooms—too few shimmering skirts;

the prayer will seem to ache
for more. But the prayer will not ache.
When we enter, its chandeliers and skies
will blush with pleasure. Inside
we will be weightless, and our goodness will not matter
in a prayer so light, so empty it will float.

SELF-PORTRAIT WITH

A BEE IN MY MOUTH

I said *no*—and then it was abuzz inside me,
all wings, restless—

Raw lust for romance—

.

You were undressing, peeling off
the thick socks you'd sweat through.

It wasn't you I'd refused.
You smelled of cut grass, your back ached,
you closed your eyes for a moment

before I kissed you in what I believed was silence.
But the buzz started up, hovered

as I searched out your lips, as I pulled you toward me,
as I *succumbed*

to the force of your lips. . . .

■

Though I kissed, of course, you,
not *the forceful domination of his lips.*

■

Like a bee in a glass jar, my mind buzzes—
But the bee is in my mouth.

■

The buzzing, sometimes, is so quiet
I don't know it's there.

I've tried to tempt it out.
Weeding the garden, I nuzzle my cheek
against the thick-veined petals, fragrances
rising like incense.
Only more fly in.

I have only to touch you to be *suddenly lifted
into the cradle of your arms*, to *surrender completely. . . .*

■

I lose you in the buzzing.

(All wings, restless,
and a kind of anger in it:
an open flower, a prairie rose
a little past bloom and still unattended—)

▪

See how close a body can come to having wings.

They pick and play me, as if I were made for them.

▪

What was I made for, then?

KEVIN YOUNG

[B. 1970]

REWARD

RUN AWAY from this sub-
scriber for the second time
are TWO NEGROES, viz. SMART,
an outlandish dark fellow

with his country marks
on his temples and bearing
the remarkable brand of my
name on his left breast, last

seen wearing an old ragged
negro cloth shirt and breeches
made of fearnought; also DIDO,
a likely young wench of a yellow

cast, born in cherrytime in this
parish, wearing a mixed coloured
coat with a bundle of clothes,
mostly blue, under her one good

arm. Both speak tolerable plain
English and may insist on being
called Cuffee and Khasa respect-
ively. Whoever shall deliver

the said goods to the gaoler
in Baton Rouge, or to the Sugar
House in the parish, shall receive
all reasonable charges plus

a genteel reward besides what
the law allows. In the mean
time all persons are strictly
forbid harbouring them, on pain

of being prosecuted to the utmost
rigour of the law. Ten guineas
will be paid to any one who can
give intelligence of their being

harboured, employed, or enter-
tained by a white person upon
his sentence; five on conviction
of a black. All Masters of vessels

are warned against carrying them
out of state, as they may claim
to be free. If any of the above
Negroes return of their own

accord, they may still be for-
given by

ELIZABETH YOUNG.

SOUTHERN UNIVERSITY, 1962

for my father

Let's see   first afros I saw   were on these girls from
            SNCC   they had dark
berets with FREEDOM NOW on them   that barely
            covered their helmets
of hair   they sang of the struggle   of the non violent
            demonstration   in town
that weekend   By Saturday it was raining like hell   me
            and Greene
we were home boys   from Opelousas High   we were
            trying to pour in
the last of the blue and white buses this black man in
            town   had let SNCC use
I had my arm in the door   trying to get on out of the
            rain   and so split my
fiveninetyfive raincoat   right down the side   I tossed it
            on the ground
and me and Greene got on just before the bus pulled
            away   When we got
outside campus ten big beefy white guys   with red
            faces and silent yellow
slickers to their knees   blocked the bus and began
            pounding and pounding
on the door with billy clubs   they tore the door off
            and stormed on

dragging the driver off the bus   throwing him in the
            trunk   they said there
wasn't gonna be no demonstration today   not here   but
            once their lights
disappeared   under all that water   someone said let's
            go   so me and Greene
and everyone else got off the anchored bus   and
            walked the four
miles to town   by our soaking selves   When we got to
            McKays   the WHITES
ONLY five&dime it was empty as a drum   they knew
            we were coming
had locked up and gone home   the street was a
            sea   of umbrellas
and soon as the wind came   which of course it
            did   my threeninetyfive
umbrella blew in on itself   so I left it on the walk   a
            broken black
bird   as we started to march towards the city
            council   Greene's fiveninety
five cardboard shoes   began falling apart   we had
            started to cross Main
Street   I could just see the top of the white marble
            building   when about
six cop cars   came wailing out of nowhere   a dozen or
            so plainclothesmen
jumped out   holding these cans of tear gas   they
            said   don't even try
crossing this street   go home and stop making

trouble   just then the light
changed   turning from red to green   we crossed   the
        men clubbed us
threw their tears at us   they took out our wallets   took
        everything we had
and left it on the sidewalk   with our streaming
        eyes   with the rain

EVENSONG

At dusk women
walking alone give off

the strangest light—
till you realize they're not—

a dark dog races
to meet one, leash

tailing; or,
a boyfriend not worth

the wait, gleeful
ungraceful, follows

far too close.
Children tire of ignoring

their mothers who half-watch
them holler. The boys

skateboarding beyond
even their bodies

have got it right—

fling yourselves, friends,
into whatever guardrail or concrete

the world has, then find
someone to get it all

down on tape.
Later, the falls will

seem obvious, about
to happen—re-wound,

the women all look
better off—and those

who fall shall stay

airborne, oblivious, halfway
to happy.

KAZIM ALI

[B. 1971]

RAIN

With thick strokes of ink the sky fills with rain.
Pretending to run for cover but secretly praying for more rain.

Over the echo of the water, I hear a voice saying my name.
No one in the city moves under the quick sightless rain.

The pages of my notebook soak, then curl. I've written:
"Yogis opened their mouths for hours to drink the rain."

The sky is a bowl of dark water, rinsing your face.
The window trembles; liquid glass could shatter into rain.

I am a dark bowl, waiting to be filled.
If I open my mouth now, I could drown in the rain.

I hurry home as though someone is there waiting for me.
The night collapses into your skin. I am the rain.

THICKET

The story unfolds like this: a blameless father
loves the as yet unharmed son.

The son is somewhat randy and alarmed
at his appearance in an orthodox world.

Does it hurt him that he's been cut from the tribe of sons
who believe, are unarmed, who recite all the rules?

It's the father who believes in God.
The son believes in the father.

The father in this story is guileless,
not trying to call God's bluff.

And unbelievably to all,
the son willingly opens his throat to the universe.

Neither one of them seeking to see Him,
not saying His name, not asking to be saved.

SAID: IN THE RAIN

Wide in the hills he came to unearth the golden tablets.
You put all this together one afternoon walking home in rain.

Last night, after playing Satie you briefly believed
the back of the mind was the only religion that mattered.

Perturbed, you never wanted words graven in fire,
but wished to be found there, buried in the hill-dirt,

in the rain, a follower of a religion of water,
and why not?

Why not be an acolyte of the twisting ribbon of river?
What else floods its way from great rock to oblivion?

In a night divided into Satie and self-evidence,
why not the religion of what always seeps back to itself?

Why not a religion of water in a time of great fires?
You fear you may drown, but your birth in it implies otherwise.

Not that it is impossible to drown, but that
this whole time you have been drowning.

STEPHEN BURT

[B. 1971]

ROAD MOVIE WITH FOOD

My atlas is soaked. And another
Thing: most sound effects in movies
Are not made on set, but in Waterford, Connecticut,
On lots, where most of the work in the world gets done.
Staid, excited back-

Seat driver, hopeful deluge
Or delusion, arriving with umbrellas
Secured under each arm, I miss you a lot:
I miss your wiles, your democratic hat
With roses up the blue side, and your faith

That people neither you nor I see have
Interior motives, that they, too, can taste
Salt in new greens, and savor the rest we crave.
Was it for this the young cooks hoped, when catkins
Hearkened to heels and currents, and gusts that branded

Dissolute meadows, and water voles
And curious, pink, endangered species of bats,
Though minor, loomed large in one another's concern?
The new lament factories all smell like braised meat.
Sleek and intestate, without a will of its own,

The stale chain of in-house rewards they might win now extends
Its braided links past Norman, Oklahoma,

Into Normal, Illinois, almost crossing
These United States from stem to stern,
Top to bottom, and back to front, once and for all.

SELF-PORTRAIT AS KITTY PRYDE

I have been identified
as gifted & dangerous. People fight over me
but not in the ways I want. Who would expect
it in a girl from Deerfield, Illinois,
town of strict zoning, no neon & quality schools?
I pass through difficult physical laws, cement,
flames, cupboards, crowds, tree trunks & arguments,
precociously, like something to protect.
I am always going through some phase.

My best friend spent apprentice years
alone inside a study like a star.
My wide eyes & Jewish hair
are shyness, a challenge to artists, &
untouchable. I can slip out of the back of a car.
When I am tired I dance, or pace
barefoot on the civilian ground
of Salem Center, where rain falls through me.
I have begun to learn to walk on air.

Adventures overemphasize my age.
In my distant & plausible future I will bear
one child, scorn, twenty-five pounds
of technology on my back, & the further weight
of giving orders to a restless band
of misfits who save America from its own rage
but cannot save themselves, & stay up late.
My friends & the fate of the world will have come to rest,
unexpected, staccato, in my sophomore hands.

OUR HISTORY

after Jaime Gil de Biedma

What else can I say about my country,
this country where the worst of the evildoers
win popularity contests, and the poor
crowd into the army, and bad government
is like the air, a faith, a way of being,
the goal and meaning of our history?

In the rickety pile of tales called history
the most ridiculous now describes our country.
Here's how it ends: as if we were one human being,
we have announced, "I'm tired of evildoers;
I'm just going to let them buy the government.
That will exhaust them. That will make them poor."

The rest of the world knows how we treat our poor:
we give them a chance to get rich. If they blow it, they're history,
and it's off to jail with them. We don't blame the government—
that's part of what we love about our country;
we're all too busy fighting evildoers
to notice the stale crusts of bread at the core of our being.

It's an old problem: how do we go on being
so comfortable, and so troubled? Are we poor
losers? Am I one of the evildoers?
Often I imagine another history,
in which our stumbling, misbegotten country
learns to tell the truth about the government;

I try, at least, to imagine that every government
simply reflects the decisions of human beings,
that no magician's curse has befallen our country—
no one has cast a spell to keep the poor
locked up, nor raised the whole dead history
of empires stretched till they snap by evildoers.

I want to believe there are no evildoers,
only men and women in government
who hold and obey their beliefs about history,
for whom buying and selling, and being
bought and sold, are no reason to send the poor
home in coffins. . . . Then I look at the country.

I too would like to be rid of the evildoers,
but for now this country likes its government.
What will the poor nations say, when they write our history?

DAN CHIASSON

[B. 1971]

DACTYLS AFTER DRIVING

THROUGH NEVADA

for J. P.

If at a party a stranger approaches,
      friend of a friend or cousin from home
O how will I greet him? Crisscrossing

      Nevada, highwayside shrines
write *wreck* in italics: one
      pilgrimage done, another begun.

What was it you said about
      guardrails, their miles and
miles of comical silence? Or road signs,

      so weird in the ultimate landscape—
the nothingness named; or what
      seems to be nothingness, canyon and

trace, evergreen grove, the rivers with
      Spanish and Indian names—
and what if that friend of a friend had a

      brother returning from Europe now
ten years ago, a brother half
      hero, half slacker, merely desires and

lovely pretensions (the *Gauloises*
    and Sartre in his carry-on
bag) turned into myth over

    Lockerbie, Scotland, spasm and
flash, suddenly any boy falling alone
    through the sky, found in a creamery?

FROM NATURAL HISTORY

GEORGIC (II)

The flowers that fade, the flowers that don't, the wax
    begonias made to look like real ones by an artisan in

Quebec, the wax insects that buzz nearby and the wax fragrance
    that attracts them, the wax lovers walking idly, their

wax promises, the entire scene done in a shoe box with a peephole
    to grant the wax lovers privacy, making your looking,

your mere looking, forbidden and therefore wonderful —
    what was that again, listen — this wax man and woman,

what disappointment is it now bows him down, as she
    half-comforts him, while her other half makes a call

on a cell phone? The flowers beam anyway, clueless.
    They ignore us—if what I mean by "us" is the wax lovers,

you and I, making a fetish of our privacy again, putting joy
    in someone's eye. And that's what I mean by us.

WHICH SPECIES ON EARTH IS SADDEST?

When we wake up in our bodies, first we weep.
    We weep because the air is thick as honey.

Even the air is a body. Ours is the bottommost
    and newest body, nested inside other, older ones

(though the mother's body is repairing itself now;
    there's no trace of us anywhere on her;

why are we part of every body but our mother's?)
    Die as soon as possible, the Scriptures say.

And many do—or soon enough, as in the tales of
    a swollen boy, now years ago, in farthest Africa,

who filled a grove of cherry trees with tears, then
    vanished into the grove. He hides behind trees.

That's death for you, a fragrant grove to hide within,
    your sister looking for you in a pile of cocaine.

That's weeping for you. Grief is a cherry grove.
    Don't be born at all. My friend is on fast-forward now

to reach the scene where they erase her childlessness.
    She knows she hid that kid somewhere inside of her,

but where? We know nothing else except by learning:
    not walking, not eating. Only to cry comes naturally.

MARY QUADE

[B. 1971]

DEATH BY FIRE

Christmas—the season for death by fire—
all warm things the flip side of tragedy—
the hearth, the stove, the string of lights
sparking. The candle—touching the tissue wrapping in her hand,
then the drapes, then—she cannot stop a thing
that wants so extravagantly. Or—needles smoldering,
almost silent. I saw the smoke,
the black stairwell, the paneless windows, the water from the hoses
frozen in blasts—this story. A holiday matinee
at the Iroquois Theater—the curtain ignites,
and the orchestra plays while the crowd leaps. We cannot stop
ourselves from shoving at locked doors. What about
Him, delivered from the flames? The bright star
leading to a savior lying in a manger
in a stable snug with beasts? So we believe in calm escape,
our divine *proof*—not our well-proven
subjection, our mundane tendency to burn.

THE LAST WILD PASSENGER PIGEON:

SERGENTS, OHIO, 1900

It's true that regret abides, but what of it?
A story needs loss, and we've all heard of the birds'
endless flock passing over, perpetual as seconds replacing
seconds—what were a few wasted? But then,
wasn't there an end, closing the tidy lesson?
A fourteen-year-old boy, the cusp of man, his sins
all curiosity, all blouses and stolen sweets, all furtive
curses, all doubts in God, all simple blood—
he sees a strange bird in the barnyard and asks his mother—
yes, a boy—for the shotgun. Innocent—
only wanting to study a still thing in death.
A local woman stuffs the bird, sews shoe buttons on for eyes—
it takes years for someone to say for certain *last*.

There are more unprecedented crimes than his; we lose
our boy to a man's designful guilts, yet even in old age
he tells of the cold morning, and the bird stops eating corn,
flaps into its tree, waiting for the boy to return with the gun—
and *there* the bird endures—and behind glass, "Buttons,"
artlessly preserved, a clumsy denouement dragging out
extinction like a sky of dark wings, like slow forgiveness.

PUBLICITY PHOTO, OPERATION CROSSROADS: MUSHROOM CLOUD CAKE

I am not an atomic playboy. —ADMIRAL W. H. P. BLANDY

A detonation of confectioner's sugar and angel food
grows from a stretch of ordinary tablecloth
out of a bed of icing braids and pompon flowers.
The wife of Admiral W. H. P. "Spike" Blandy holds her hand
like a glove digesting bones
over the Admiral's own. She has sliced cakes before,
knows how to pull the wedge from the whole,
work a piece gently so as not to lose the tip,
leave an attractive gash. The Admiral has spoken,
or is about to speak, his mouth unclosed,
his head unstable on his neck. She was perhaps lovely
before her face became a thin box
for the display of hats.

When the picture hits the papers, priests across the country
erupt in conscientious outrage—
such mockery of apocalypse—
as if they knew nothing of celebrations
of death and miracle. Of course,
the cake is tasteless.
A week before, a patriotic baker in Illinois

sifts his flour into a bowl,
separates two dozen eggs; the yolks, two dozen suns;
the whites, whipped into peaks; the bakery air,
a fog of sweetness as something rises in the heat.

KATRINA VANDENBERG

[B. 1971]

THE FLOATING

When he was dying, she stayed with him all night,
but one night, restless, she walked around a corner
and found a dim hall full of children's breathing
rising from small white beds. She had drifted
into the Floating, the children's hospital boat
being rocked to sleep in the harbor again
the way it was a hundred summers ago.
The horizon of her life had vanished—traffic
lights, students with Chinese takeout boxes
stories down. Now bustled dresses drooped
over the backs of chairs; now immigrant mothers
in flimsy shifts bent over the beds and whispered,
tendrils of hair escaping their tidy knots,
their feet unsteady on the pitch of breath.

MARRIAGE PORTRAIT OF THE ARNOLFINIS

In the mirror behind the merchant groom and bride, I've seen
the two extra figures: the artist and me—or you.
The bride's high-waisted green dress is medieval,

their faces flat, and yet that mirror is *modern*,
        demanding we look outside the frame. Look
at the way the artist signs his name above it,

        Jan van Eyck was here, the final sentence
of an age of anonymous art for God.
        We witness Bruges in 1434. The mirror's an eye.

How else can we get in, make sense of people
        as foreign to us as Arnolfini? Think of him,
his gestures too broad for lanterned tavern tables,

        the deals he cuts on cloth while littering the floor
with mussel shells. His tongue an eel strangling
        Flemish verbs. Welcome to the city

where Arnolfini is lost most of the time.
        When he walks over bridges to the wharf at night,
the shut-eyed houses look the same, all cut

        from gingerbread. If there's a moon,
a second city rises in the canals —
        Venezia, with its marzipan domes, mosaics,

mirrors. Did Arnolfini feel that he lived nowhere,
        his world a port whose canals and bridges
reflect each other? Rotterdam, Antwerp,

Marseilles, Genova . . . was trade the only metaphor
he understood; for instance, did he think,
        when he arranged to have his portrait done,

that the Flemish did light better than the Italians,
        in spite of the rain, because their sun's a rare
gold coin? Because of what Low Country workers do.

        Without materials of their own, in a country born
of the sea and will, they import all they need—
        wool, hops, and Baltic logs. Even the stones that become

their churches are hauled in wagons from France.
        In their hands wool is cloth, and hops are beer,
and logs turn into ships with bellies full

        of cloves and cinnamon. So clay is tiles.
And light is art. *What a strange country,*
        Arnolfini may have thought. What people,

I say, centuries away, to turn
        the raw stuff of life into goods that anyone
might own and use. Thank you, van Eyck,

        for your eye, this marriage. I take this mirror
to be my bridge. I take this day in Bruges.
        I will love and honor you all of my days. I do.

HUNGER WINTER

Haarlem, 1944

In the end, the ones who live
do so on a rationed piece
of bread, a potato, and one
sugar beet a day. They thicken
their broth with newspaper, butcher
the cat. An old woman queues
in her patched shoes
all afternoon for seed potatoes
and tulip bulbs broken
from the frozen ground. At home,
she slices them for *hutspot*,
the bulbs like shallots, the crackle
of their papery skins answering
the questions of the stove fire
that burns an empty cupboard.
That night for dinner
the woman swallows the spring,
which tastes like sweetened
chestnuts. Eighteen thousand
of the Dutch will die that winter,
including the woman. The bulbs
and seed potatoes will be
among the last to go: the hope,
the strength to wait for the weather

to turn. The time when the bulbs
enter the familiar belly
of the dark, they will not rise
when the sun calls their names.
They will not nod *yes*
in the red fields of Lisse
where the old woman bicycled
with a boy in April, long ago.

RACHEL ZUCKER

[B. 1971]

LETTER [PERSEPHONE TO DEMETER]

At home, the bells were a high light-yellow
with no silver or gray just buttercup or sugar-and-lemon.

Here bodies are lined in blue against the sea.
And where red is red there is only red.

I have to be blue to bathe in the sea.
Red, to live in the red room with red air

to rest my head, red cheek down, on the red table.

Above, it was so green: brown, yellow, white, green.
My longing for red furious, sexual.

There things were alive but nothing moved.
Now I live near the sea in a place which has no blue and is not the sea.

Gulls flock, leeward then tangent
and pigeons bully them off the ground.

Hardly alive, almost blind—a hot geometry casts off
every color of the world. Everything moves, nothing alive.

In the red room there is a sky which is painted over in red
but is not red and was, once, the sky.

This is how I live.

THISTLE, OR LETTER FOR MY HUSBAND (33 WEEKS)

Do you have a spare self or shadow to keep me cool
take off this dreadful skin, future pressing in, the present humid,
   slippery
you know your wife too big used to be me but I espy your dream
of women never thin enough   if I could photograph myself
out of this, be a man writing about animals or history, extinct fauna,
husked mollusks but I can't. Look how the months swing by and
   taunt me—

                                     Oh! I'm attached!
one day will be a cloth monkey—but I swear, I will not be done to.
I will not be a smooth oyster waiting for nacre to coat my unseens,
   despair
polishing, bending light through me. Instead I'd sell my long hair
for a few mother-of-pearl buttons, unclasp my heart from its open
   birdcage
but not put desire away, I'll not put desire away. Remember: I am
   inside who I was.

THE DESSERTS WILL MAKE YOU
STUPID WITH HAPPINESS

It used to be that generations died for nothing
but old age or, otherwise, tragedy. We have
no right to address history. No right to prefer
a father to a mother. A husband to a friend.

Peaches over plums. For so began the bombings.
Let the slamming door miss your close attention.
If he dresses his heart with mayonnaise instead of
lemon-butter it is none of your business. This

sickness of looking proves addictive. It eclipses
slavery, suffrage, the chambers. Meanwhile,
I wear my own hair without a thought. I make
lists of the damned and outside, they all change

jobs. I watch through binoculars as they all
change jobs. An infant screams the double-bleating
wail of hunger, then quiets when a breast appears
from somewhere. Just another ice cream truck

under the window. Planes keeping the sky
involved. Women losing weight after the first
child. By now too many people have touched
all the fruits and vegetables so no one knows

how the drug got out of vials they were saving
for special occasions. We just suddenly noticed
everything dusted in saffron but still so inexpensive.
Ask your father what his father did for a living—

what happened when the factories were converted.
How they all made money back in the day,
back in the days when the brown bettys were good
though the apples looked less perfect.

LISA OLSTEIN

[B. 1972]

BLUE WARP BLACK WEAVE

It happened because somewhere a wind died down.
I stopped loving you when a pebble hit the windshield.
A moth at the window is a symbol.

I stopped loving you when you asked me to.
A moth at the door is a sign. It would have
happened if she'd filled her pockets with stones.

It wouldn't have happened if she'd waited
one second more. I started loving you
when your sleeve caught fire. I started loving you

in a boat at sea. When it happens, how long before
a crowd accumulates, people and pigeons lining the curb?
How long before we can gauge the tensile strength

of the moment, some place where it breaks?
One man's meat, another's treason.
One man's trash, another's each-to-his-own.

One snow, suddenly birds are twice their usual size,
feather coats puffed around them, coming up
with mouthfuls of sometimes seed, sometimes snow.

ANOTHER STORY WITH
A BURNING BARN IN IT

I was on the porch pinching back the lobelia
like trimming a great blue head of hair.

We'd just planted the near field, the far one
the day before. I'd never seen it so clear,

so gusty, so overcast, so clear, so calm.
They say pearls must be worn or they lose their luster,

and that morning I happened to remember,
so I put them on for milking, finding some

sympathy, I guess, between the two.
Usually I don't sit down until much later in the day.

The lobelia was curling in the sun. One by one
birds flew off, and that should have been a sign.

Trust is made and broken. I hardly sit down
at all. It was the time of year for luna moths,

but we hadn't had any yet settling on the porch
or hovering above the garden I'd let the wild rose take.

STEADY NOW

In swaths of blood-soaked bandages
poppies sway across the plain.
Birds thrust down their wings,
stick out their beaks, and follow one another
until something makes them fly away—
flame-blue heads in glancing sun.

Each year even the smallest pass us
on their way south, and months later
flying north again. For them,
the heart beats fast and the body is a furnace.
For us, the body is a window, a doorstop,
a weighty parcel on the back of a mare.

Butterflies, too, pass us on their long relays to and from.
Once in an ice storm not meant for May,
we watched hundreds freeze on night branches.
In the morning they drifted like embers,
bright fragments collecting around the horses' mouths
whenever they dipped their heads to the ground.

TRACY K. SMITH

[B. 1972]

THIRST

The old man they called Bagre
Who welcomed us with food
And rice-paper cigarettes
At the table outside his cabin
Was the one who told the soldiers
To sit down. They were drunk.
They'd seen the plates on our car
From the road and came to where
You and I and Bagre and his son
Sat laughing. I must have been
Drunk myself to laugh so hard
At what I didn't understand.

It was night by then. We smoked
To keep off the mosquitoes.
There was fish to eat—nothing but fish
Bagre and the other men caught.
The two little girls I'd played with
Were asleep in their hammocks.
Even Genny and Manuel,
Who rode with us and waited
While we hurried out of our clothes
And into those waves the color
Of atmosphere.

Before the soldiers sat down,
They stood there, chests ballooned.

When we showed them our papers,
They wanted something else.
One of them touched the back of my leg.
With your eyes, you told me
To come beside you. There were guns
Slung over their shoulders
Like tall sticks. They stroked them
Absently with their fingers.

Their leader was called Jorge.
I addressed him in the familiar.
I gave him a half-empty bottle
Of what we were drinking.
When it was empty, I offered to fill it
With water from the cooler.
He took a sip, spat it out
And called you by your name.
I didn't want to see you
Climb onto that jeep of theirs—so tall
And broad it seemed they'd ridden in
On elephants yoked shoulder to shoulder,
Flank to flank.

Maybe this is a story
About the old man they called Bagre.
The one with the crooked legs
That refused to run.
Maybe this is a story about being too old
To be afraid, and too young not to fear

Authority, and abuse it, and call it
By its name, and call it a liar.
Or maybe it's a story about the fish.
The ones hanging on branches
To dry, and the ones swimming
With eyes that would not shut
In water that entered them
And became them
And kept them from thirst.

MANGOES

The woman in a blouse
The color of daylight
Motions to her daughter not to slouch.
They wait without luggage.
They have been waiting
Since before the station smelled
Of cigarettes. Shadows
Fill the doorway and fade
One by one
Into bloated faces.
She'd like to swat at them
Like the lazy flies
That swarm her kitchen.

She considers her hands, at rest
Like pale fruits in her lap. Should she
Gather them in her skirt and hurry
Down the tree in reverse, greedy
For a vivid mouthful of something
Sweet? The sun gets brighter
As it drops low. Soon the room
Will glow gold with late afternoon.
Still no husband, face creased from sleep,
His one bag across his chest. Soon
The windows will grow black. Still
No one with his hand always returning
To the hollow below her back.

Desire is a city of yellow houses
As it surrenders its drunks to the night.
It is the drunks on ancient bicycles
Warbling into motionless air,
And the pigeons, asleep in branches,
That will repeat the same songs tomorrow
Believing them new. Desire is the woman
Awake now over a bowl of ashes
That flutter and drop like abandoned feathers.
It's the word *widow* spelled slowly in air
With a cigarette that burns
On its own going.

FROM JOY

It will rain tomorrow, as it rained in the days after you died.
And I will struggle with what to wear, and take a place on the bus
Among those I will only ever know by the shape their shoulders make
Above the backs of the seats before mine. It is November,

And storm clouds ascend above the roofs outside my window.
I don't know anymore where you've gone to. Whether your soul
Waits here—in my room, in the kitchen with the newly blown bulb—
Or whether it rose instantly to the kingdom of hosannas. Some nights,

Walking up my steps in the dark, digging for the mail and my keys,
I know you are far, infinitely far from us. That you watch
In the way one of us might pause a moment to watch a frenzy of ants,
Wanting to help, to pick up the crumb and put it down
Close to their hill, seeing their purpose that clearly.

QUAN BARRY

[B. 1973]

ASYLUM

The fish are the first to return:
the moorish idol, the black surgeon,

the trumpet and lesser scorpion, the angel
seemingly radiogenic, the goatfish

with its face of spikes. Whole phyla converging:
the devil rays in fluid sheets, the leatherbacks,

hawksbills, their shells reticent as maps.
On the atoll: the golden plover, the kingfisher,

egrets and honeyeaters
nesting like an occupation. And the flowers:

the flame trees, the now forgotten, the wait-a-bit
all drawn to what we desert, a preserve

where the chinese lantern's elliptic seed
is bone-smooth, cesium-laced.

VISITOR

In hindsight the amazing thing wasn't her surviving
but the fact that a stranger entered her room.

Of course it's all supposition, nothing
too convicting. Perhaps they struggled.

Maybe he simply ordered her supine.
All they uncovered: a locked house, her bedroom door

slightly ajar, approximately four pints staining
her pillow, a one inch section atop the crown of her head

crushed as finely as herbs. Three days later
the paperweight came back from the lab

sticky with an unreadable palm, almost as if
someone were cupping it, racing to beat

a stack of papers before they stirred.
I'm not making this up. She was my sister's best friend,

a teen with more than a hundred sutures
embedded in her scalp. Like a dead tree she went on,

maintaining she remembered nothing
about the incident, each night

sleeping behind the same door
across from his, desperate to believe

in the official version, in planned randomness.
I can't tell you her name, I won't tell you

because it's all you'll remember, you'll lie down at night
thinking it doesn't apply.

DOUG FLUTIE'S 1984 ORANGE BOWL
HAIL MARY AS WATER INTO FIRE

Listen w/o distraction.

Even before its incarnation we were transported, which is to say
    we were there, the Miami night
      larval, charged.

Read this to me when I'm dying, when I'm in the intermediate
    state—my consciousness dissipating through the elements.

Did the child-me know it would be all right, that the next six seconds
    would represent human existence?

This is the way it always begins: in huddled confusion, then the
    object churning toward a predetermined end.

There is a plan. There is hope. Then something happens.

Love comes & goes. Anger. Happiness. Decay. A man stands on the
    other side & holds out his hands.

Something is sailing through the new year.

Teacher, call me by my other name. Tell me to breathe through my
    eyes, see the path through the luminosity.

We are the ball. We are the arc through the air. We are the no time left
    on the clock & the disbeliever.

Read this to me when I'm dying, when I'm neither here
    nor there.

Say, "Grab onto nothing & it will come to you."

AIMEE NEZHUKUMATATHIL

[B. 1974]

GULABJAMOON JAR

I love saying the name. Each sweet syllable seems like there ought to be a crush of sugar on your tongue, a tiny reward just for saying the word. These soft milk-balls, fried golden and soaked in sugar syrup, are glassed up in a luxuriously oversized jar that my grandmother collects under her spice table to store homemade mango and spicy lime pickles. But for Uncle Jacob, these jars serve as seasonal aquariums. When I asked him where the fish in the gulabjamoon jar (now sitting in the center of his dining table) came from, he said *after rain, these fish appear in road puddles.* Uncle asked a boy to catch some in a towel: a present for my aunt. These fish are small, two inches long. A black teardrop shape behind each eye, and again, if you didn't catch it the first time, on the tail. Odd because they don't have the traditional fish 'shape,' where the body tapers into a kissy mouth and ends in a swish of tail — more like little silver rectangles suspended in the jar. Uncle said when the puddles dry up in the sun, the fish aren't there to crack and split their smooth milkskins. He's never yet seen one dead in the street. Like the fish knew they had to move to a new wet place. Perhaps they were snatched up by a dog or pecked to bits by a rooster. All over the village, wet dogs and wet chickens roam the moss-covered alleys. Nobody knows who cares for these animals but all of them have a crafty gleam in their eye that says: *Yes, I ate more than even you today.* On the table, the fish watch me watch them eat rice, the only food my aunt gives them. I see the rice fluff in their bellies, swelling. I tap the jar with a fork and the only response is a slight shift in their togetherness — a white square of silk thrown into a small sea.

CROW JOY

Almost all of the gold leaf on the Kremlin domes was scratched off years ago from the fleet of crows converging at the top. Contrary to popular belief, they were not stealing the shiny flakes for their nests, as they would a lovely kerchief pinned too loose on a clothesline, or withered breadfruit left too long in sun. A closer look revealed their game of sliding down those onion domes, their claws scraping the roofskin raw. In sunlight, crow wings flash a wild blue, as blue as the nose of a jolly mandrill. Half a world away, a family of these monkeys dips their fingers into a stream for the first time—their black fingernails dulled square for scratching stems to drink, their noses wet, warm. A shopkeeper near the *Lobnoye Mesto*, The Place of Skulls, once recorded distressed crow calls to scare the birds from their play. But the top was too high or the tape too quiet—the birds' feet already too gilded to ever want to step foot on this earth again.

MAKING GYOTAKU

In Osaka, fishermen have no use for the brag,
the frantic gestures of length, blocks of air

between their hands. They flatten their catch
halfway into a tray of sand, steady

the slick prize. The nervous quiver
of the artist's hands over the fish —washing it

with dark ink, careful not to spill or waste,
else feel the wrath of salty men long at sea.

If it is a good print, the curves and channels of each scale
will appear as tidy patterns to be framed and hung

in the hallway of his house. But perhaps the gesture
I love most —before the pressing of rice paper over

inked fish, before the gentle peel away of the print
to show the fish's true size —is the quick-light stroke

of the artist's thumb, how deftly he wipes away
the bit of black ink from the fish's jelly eye —

how he lets it look back from the wall at the villagers,
the amazed staring back at the amazed.

BEN LERNER

[B. 1979]

FROM *THE LICHTENBERG FIGURES*

Your child lacks a credible god-term, a jargon of ultimacy.
He fails to distinguish between illusion (*Schein*) and beautiful
    illusion (*schöner Schein*).
He is inept and unattractive.
Today I asked your child to depress

the right pedal, to stop the action of the dampers
so that the strings could vibrate freely. In response he struck me
in the stomach with a pipe.

Your child is a bereavement arbitrarily prescribed,
a hyperkinetic disorder expressed in chromatic variations.
By the age of twenty-three, your child will be bald
and dead. He's a bright boy and eager to learn. But bourgeois
    spectator forms

have supplanted the music of the salon,
inciting a sheer vertical sonority
that has dispatched the theme to keys beyond his reach.

FROM *THE LICHTENBERG FIGURES*

The sky narrates snow. I narrate my name in the snow.
Snow piled in paragraphs. Darkling snow. Geno-snow
and pheno-snow. I staple snow to the ground.

In medieval angelology, there are nine orders of snow.
A vindication of snow in the form of snow.
A jealous snow. An omni-snow. Snow immolation.

Do you remember that winter it snowed?
There were bodies everywhere. Obese, carrot-nosed.
A snow of translucent hexagonal signifiers. Meta-snow.

Sand replaced with snow. Snowpaper. A window of snow
opened onto the snow. Snow replaced with sand.
A sandman. Obese, carrot-nosed. Tiny swastikas

of snow. Vallejo's unpublished snow.
Real snow on the stage. Fake blood on the snow.

FROM *ANGLE OF YAW*

When night falls in the middle west we divide the multiple fruit of the pig. A drunk man calls out for traditional shepherds' music addressing the theme of love, scratch that, the theme of boredom. The children are made to recite the Office of the Shutting of the Eyes. The saltshaker is full of pepper. The peppershaker: glitter. At the bottom of every drained pool, there I are. There we am, openmouthed, awaiting the small, angular rain. A drunk man brews a second cup, one for each fist. Great tufts of white carpet pulled out in grief, scratch that, in boredom. In the planar region bounded by our counterglow, no means no. So does yes. Everything we own is designed to be easily washed, unlike the aprons of the butchers that we are.

LILAH HEGNAUER

[B. 1982]

TEACH ANYTHING

Teach anything, the headmaster told me;
he didn't return for five weeks. Clueless
as a gift chicken, I slowly learned
our lessons: they didn't know about

the slave trade, Martin Luther King, snow,
informal greetings, Shakespeare. Everything
was new, the world of English burst forth
tart on their palates: verbs, nouns,

conjugation of tenses. Amanyire whispered
to Mukabalisa, "Whatever you choose to claim
of me is always yours, *nkwagala*;" I dropped
my jaw. My hands and their papers dropped.

English infiltrated their romance. I can't
understand my body turning toward them,
turning away, turning again, and finally away;
English, Luganda, they're speaking Luzungu.

I learn each evening, roasting maize on charcoal,
language doesn't matter when it comes to love.
Like yellow kernels taking on the heat,
gradually we all want to be printed upon.

If I could sink myself into this ink and write myself
onto a page I would lie down in what they taught me
about iambs: walk under a full moon to the latrine—don't
light the lantern, leave it next to the sleeper.

Go later in the month when the moon is a hair, don't
light the lantern, fumble to the pit and back into bed.
Teach anything. Print the way upon your mind
until it's all sensory, all footpath-thin, all charted loam.

KATENDE PASSION FRUIT
AND GROUNDNUTS

Grafted, a yellow to purple hybrid, the yellow
lives longer, gives more fruit, but oh, the purple
is so sweet that the compromise is worth the loss
of longevity, the only reason for our hybrid fruit—
utility took taste for wife but it makes a poor shade
as I sat plucking groundnuts with Kabooi.

When I came to help, he cleared a space on the mat
and turned his body on splayed knees to face me.
His trousers were cuffed higher than I remember,
his fingers were bent to the raw nuts, his
eyebrows thick over a disquiet face. Kabooi, they

call him or he calls himself; Cowboy, I used to say
because he tends the cows. "You are married,"

he said, with that look older men often give me,
wondering how long I'll stay and why I'm here.
I'm not marriageable, I tried to say—but am lost at
how to tell him of my own grafting; instead, I
grabbed a clump of dirt and nuts and harvested with
Kabooi deep into the evening until the sky
was a plowed mix of orange and blue.

IMMUNIZING IN BUKOBA

1.

Ninety-four women gathered with their babies
on 11 June 2003 in the village of Bukoba
in Mubende district for polio, tetanus, tuberculosis,
diptheria, hepatitis B, and whooping cough vaccinations.

There was a woman with a pale green scarf
tied around her shaved head, waiting on the first bench.
When her baby started to pee, she set it on the dirt floor
between her feet. When he was done, she picked him up
and opened her *gomesi* to nurse him on cracked nipples.

We laid the needles and pills out at a school,
sent the teacher and his students in
thin blue shirts and dresses home for the day
so we could use their space to weigh babies and vaccinate.
The girls fourteen and older stayed because
they are childbearing age and need tetanus vaccines.

The woman, 17, whose second child, 3 months old,
weighed just under 4 kilos and drooled down my dress
as I bent over to place him in the suspended shorts
for weighing, was later bent over her son, singing
in Luganda and restraining him during the tetanus shot.

III.

The roof of the schoolhouse had holes in the thatching
to let light in. The brickwork was crumbling
and children tumbled around the holes
to see their first glimpse of *Bazungu*.

The woman with the pale yellow *gomesi*, Naalongo,
with twin girls, 11 months old, didn't know their birth date,
their birth weight, or the spelling of her name.
They walked from Kyiya at dawn and left Bukoba at 7.

IV.

The blackboards were pieced from bits,
the dirt floors swept bare. There were
no desks and the benches splintered and bowed.

The woman with a short neck and broad nose curving
toward her lips handed her screaming son to me
for weighing; as he caught sight of my face
he stopped crying and reached his hands to my glasses.

V.

Outside the schoolhouse, a game of soccer was
going on; barefoot with a ball of rags,
children chased through the oncoming dusk
like raindrops dancing on a cowhide drum.

There was a woman, thirty years old, who had
lost three children to AIDS and brought her infant
for vaccination. Her husband saw a prostitute
and brought back the promise of her early grave
after eight months of marriage. Her lips
are the only full part of her left and they are thick,
fading into her mouth a deep menstrual red.

VI.

I crouched over the pit latrine at midday,
the sun radiating through the thatching
just above my head. Standing up, I nearly
knocked the low cover over; I made myself
a shunt to the roof as I let my skirt back down.

A broad-shouldered woman, Proscovia, twenty years old,
brought her son, Kevina Kawgu, two months old.
His belly button was protruding three centimeters
and there was a ring of raw skin around his neck
and sores in his mouth. His eyeballs were distended
(though not as much as his mother's) and he had
lesions on his eyelids. His tonsils were white and
swollen and his arms were covered in scabs.

VII.

Through the crowd, Joyce the midwife weaves a way
from woman to woman to give iron tablets
and listen for heartbeats and tell the young women
to push when it comes time. Joyce lost six grown children
to AIDS and now cares for her grandkids; she tells
one woman to pray for twins and eat more avocados.

Nakalanzi Lucia's son, Luke Ndayambazi, was three months old.
They walked from Kawci. She knows her other children
have syphilis and now Luke's bald scalp is covered in sores
and he won't nurse. The injections are five hundred shillings each.

VIII.

Under the coming moon, a woman grabbed her
infant by the wrist and swung him around
her body to her back as she hunched forward
and tied the traveling cloth around first over her
breasts and then around her waist. Standing up
she reached behind to shift him into place.

There was a pregnant woman who looked bigger
than the rest; Sister Pascazia predicted twins.
The woman's face opened wide as she turned
looking over her shoulder, revealing a neck of
tendons and skin so tight that the lines of her
throat cartilage showed under her jaw.

WILLIAM MEREDITH

[1919–2007]

THE ILLITERATE

Touching your goodness, I am like a man
Who turns a letter over in his hand
And you might think this was because the hand
Was unfamiliar but, truth is, the man
Has never had a letter from anyone;
And now he is both afraid of what it means
And ashamed because he has no other means
To find out what it says than to ask someone.

His uncle could have left the farm to him,
Or his parents died before he sent them word,
Or the dark girl changed and want him for beloved.
Afraid and letter-proud, he keeps it with him.
What would you call his feeling for the words
That keep him rich and orphaned and beloved?

NOTES ON THE POEMS

Juliana Spahr, "Gathering: Palolo Stream": This poem references the Hawaii Supreme Court's opinion *Public Access Shoreline Hawai'i v. Hawai'i County Planning Commission*, 1995 WL 515898. The opinion protects indigenous Hawaiians' traditional and customary rights of access to gather plants, harvest trees, and take game. In this decision, the court said about the balance between the rights of private landowners and the rights of persons exercising traditional Hawaiian culture that "the western concept of exclusivity is not universally applicable in Hawai'i." A 1997 attempt by state legislators to regulate the law provoked large protests and was not passed. These rights, however, are constantly eroded by property owners who restrict physical access by fencing in areas, closing roads, diverting water, etc.

Natasha Trethewey: These poems, from Trethewey's 2002 collection, *Bellocq's Ophelia*, are written in the imagined voice of Ophelia, an unnamed prostitute photographed in New Orleans circa 1912 by E. J. Bellocq.

Honorée Fanonne Jeffers, "Outlandish Blues": The epigraph is taken from Michael A. Gomez's book, *Exchanging Our Country Marks: The Transformation of African Identities in the Colonial and Antebellum South*, 1998. The quote references a passage from George W. Mullin's *Flight and Rebellion: Slave Resistance in Eighteenth Century Virginia*, 1972.

Jenny Factor, "Riqueza": This epigraph features four lines from Chilean writer Gabriela Mistral's poem of the same title. The source is Doris Dana's bilingual volume, *The Selected Poems of Gabriela Mistral*, 1961.

Dan Chiasson, "Georgic (II)" and "Which Species on Earth Is Saddest?": These two poems are from the sequence entitled "Natural History," inspired in part by the *Historia Naturalis* of Pliny the Elder.

BIOGRAPHICAL NOTES

SHERMAN ALEXIE was born in Wellpinit, Washington in 1966. He is the author of numerous books of fiction and poetry, including *One Stick Song* (2000), *The Summer of Black Widows* (1996), and *The Business of Fancydancing* (1991). He lives and works in Seattle, Washington.

KAZIM ALI was born in Croydon, England in 1971. He is the author of two poetry collections, *The Fortieth Day* (2008) and *The Far Mosque* (2005), and a novel, *Quinn's Passage* (2004). He teaches at Oberlin College in Ohio and in the Stonecoast MFA program of the University of Southern Maine.

CRAIG ARNOLD was born in California in 1967. W. S. Merwin chose his first book, *Shells* (1999), for the Yale Series of Younger Poets, and his second collection, *Made Flesh*, is forthcoming in 2008. He teaches at the University of Wyoming in Laramie, where he lives with his son.

QUAN BARRY was born in Saigon, Vietnam in 1973, and was raised on Boston's North Shore. She is the author of *Controvertibles* (2004) and *Asylum* (2001), which won the Agnes Lynch Starrett Poetry Prize. She teaches at the University of Wisconsin.

STEPHEN BURT, born in Baltimore, Maryland in 1971, grew up in and around Washington, DC. He is the author of *Parallel Play* (2006) and *Popular Music* (1999), and of several books of literary criticism, most recently *The Forms of Youth: 20th-Century Poetry and Adolescence* (2007). He teaches at Harvard University in Massachusetts.

DAN CHIASSON was born in Burlington, Vermont in 1971. He is the author of two books of poems, *Natural History* (2005) and *The Afterlife of Objects* (2002), and a book of criticism, *One Kind of Everything* (2006). He teaches at Wellesley College in Massachusetts.

MORRI CREECH was born in Moncks Corner, South Carolina in 1970. He is the author of *Field Knowledge* (2005), winner of the Anthony Hecht Poetry

Prize, and *Paper Cathedrals* (2001), winner of the Stan and Tom Wick Poetry Prize. He lives in Lake Charles, Louisiana and teaches at McNeese State University.

JENNY FACTOR was born in New Haven, Connecticut in 1969. She is the author of *Unraveling at the Name* (2002), which was a finalist for the Lambda Literary Award. She serves on the core faculty in poetry at Antioch University Los Angeles.

LILAH HEGNAUER was born in Puyallup, Washington in 1982. She is the author of *Dark Under Kiganda Stars* (2005), which won an honorable mention for the 2006 Library of Virginia Literary Award. Hegnauer is a recipient of an Astraea Lesbian Writers Grant. She lives in Charlottesville, Virginia.

H. L. HIX [EDITOR] was born in Stillwater, Oklahoma in 1960. He is the author of five collections of poetry, most recently *God Bless: A Political/Poetic Discourse* (2007) and *Chromatic* (2006), a finalist for the National Book Award for Poetry. He has edited *Wild and Whirling Words: A Poetic Conversation* (2004), and collaborated on translations of Estonian and Lithuanian poetry. He is a professor in the creative writing MFA program at the University of Wyoming.

HONORÉE FANONNE JEFFERS was born in Kokomo, Indiana in 1967. She has published three books of poetry, the most recent of which is *Red Clay Suite* (2007) and she is a winner of a Rona Jaffe Foundation Writers' Award. She is a professor at the University of Oklahoma.

DEVIN JOHNSTON, born in 1970, was raised in North Carolina. He is the author of *Aversions* (2004), *Telepathy* (2001), and a critical study, *Precipitations: Contemporary American Poetry as Occult Practice* (2002). He teaches at St. Louis University, Missouri.

BHANU KAPIL was born in London in 1968. A British-Indian writer, she lives in Colorado, where she teaches writing at Naropa University. She is the author of three full-length collections: *The Vertical Interrogation of Strangers* (2001), *Incubation: a space for monsters* (2006), and the forthcoming *Humanimal [a project for future children]*.

DAVID KEPLINGER was born in Norristown, Pennsylvania in 1968. His third collection, *The Prayers of Others* (2006), won the Colorado Book Award. New Issues recently published his translations of Danish poet Carsten René Nielsen, *World Cut Out with Crooked Scissors*. He teaches at American University in Washington, DC.

BEN LERNER was born in Topeka, Kansas in 1979. He is the author of *Angle of Yaw* (2006), a finalist for the National Book Award, and *The Lichtenberg Figures* (2004). A former Fulbright scholar in Madrid, Spain, he co-founded and co-edits *No: a journal of the arts*, and now lives in Pittsburgh, Pennsylvania.

WILLIAM MEREDITH was born in New York City in 1919. His first book, *Love Letter from an Impossible Land* (1944), won the Yale Series of Younger Poets Award. His book *Partial Accounts* (1987) won the Pulitzer Prize and his *Effort at Speech* (1997) won the National Book Award. He died in 2007.

AIMEE NEZHUKUMATATHIL was born in Chicago in 1974. She is the author of *At the Drive-In Volcano* (2007) and *Miracle Fruit* (2003). A former Middlebrook Fellow at the Wisconsin Institute for Creative Writing, she is now associate professor of English at the State University of New York Fredonia.

LISA OLSTEIN was born in Boston in 1972. She is the author of *Radio Crackling, Radio Gone* (2006), winner of the Hayden Carruth Award, and *Cloud Hands*, forthcoming in 2009. She co-founded the Juniper Initiative for Literary Arts and Action, and is the associate director of the University of Massachusetts Amherst MFA Program.

KEVIN PRUFER was born in 1969 in Cleveland, Ohio. He is the author of *National Anthem* (2008), *Fallen from a Chariot* (2005), and *The Finger Bone* (2002), among others. The recipient of three Pushcart prizes, he lives in Missouri, where he edits *Pleiades: A Journal of New Writing*.

MARY QUADE was born in Frederick, Maryland in 1971. She is the author of *Guide to Native Beasts* (2003). In 2001, she was awarded an Oregon Literary Fellowship. In 2006, she received an Ohio Arts Council Individual Excellence Award. She teaches at Hiram College in Ohio.

PAISLEY REKDAL was born in Seattle, Washington in 1970. She is the author of *The Invention of the Kaleidoscope* (2007), *Six Girls Without Pants* (2002), and *A Crash of Rhinos* (2000). She received a Fulbright fellowship in 1996 and now teaches at the University of Utah.

TRACY K. SMITH was born in Falmouth, Massachusetts in 1972. She is the author of *Duende* (2007), which received the 2006 James Laughlin Award from the Academy of American Poets, and *The Body's Question* (2003), winner of the 2002 Cave Canem Poetry Prize. She teaches at Princeton University in New Jersey and lives in Brooklyn, New York.

JULIANA SPAHR was born in Chillicothe, Ohio in 1966. She is the author of *This Connection of Everyone with Lungs* (2005), *Fuck You—Aloha—I Love You* (2001), and *Response* (1996), a winner of a National Poetry Series prize. She currently lives in Berkeley, California, in a house that was once rented to Mario Savio.

WILLIAM STAFFORD was born in Hutchinson, Kansas in 1914. He published more than sixty volumes of poetry and prose, and received the National Book Award, a Guggenheim Fellowship, and the Western States Lifetime Achievement Award in Poetry. In 1970, he was the consultant in poetry to the U.S. Library of Congress. He died in 1993.

A. E. STALLINGS was born in 1968 and raised in Decatur, Georgia. She is the author of *Hapax* (2006) and *Archaic Smile* (1999). She has received the Frederick Bock Prize, the Richard Wilbur Award, and the Howard Nemerov Sonnet Award. She now lives in Athens, Greece.

DONNA STONECIPHER was born in Seattle, Washington in 1969. She is a graduate of the Iowa Writers' Workshop and the author of *The Cosmopolitan*, preselected as winner of a 2007 National Poetry Series prize. She also wrote *Souvenir de Constantinople* (2007) and *The Reservoir* (2002). She has lived in Tehran and Prague, and now splits her time between Berlin, Germany and Athens, Georgia.

MARY SZYBIST was born in Williamsport, Pennsylvania in 1970. She is the author of *Granted* (2003), which was a finalist for the National Book Critics Circle Award. The recipient of the Beatrice Hawley Award and a Rona Jaffe Foundation Writers' Award, she teaches at Lewis & Clark College in Portland, Oregon.

DIANE THIEL was born in Coral Gables, Florida in 1967. She is the author of six books of poetry and nonfiction, including *Resistance Fantasies* (2004) and *Echolocations* (2000). A recipient of the Robert Frost and Robinson Jeffers awards and a recent Fulbright scholar, she is a professor at the University of New Mexico.

NATASHA TRETHEWEY was born in Mississippi in 1966. She is the author of *Native Guard* (2006), winner of the Pulitzer Prize, *Bellocq's Ophelia* (2002), and *Domestic Work* (1999), winner of the Cave Canem Poetry Prize. She teaches at Emory University in Atlanta, Georgia.

KATRINA VANDENBERG was born in Detroit, Michigan in 1971. She is the author of *Atlas* (2004) and the recipient of fellowships from the McKnight, Bush, and Fulbright foundations. She lives in Saint Paul, Minnesota.

CHRISTIAN WIMAN was born in Texas in 1966. He is the author of *Hard Night* (2005) and *The Long Home* (1998), winner of the Nicholas Roerich Poetry Prize, as well as an essay collection, *Ambition and Survival: Becoming a Poet* (2007). He lives in Chicago where he serves as editor of *Poetry* magazine.

KEVIN YOUNG was born in 1970. He is the author of *For the Confederate Dead* (2007), *Jelly Roll: A Blues* (2003), *To Repel Ghosts* (2001), and *Most Way Home* (1995), a winner of the National Poetry Series. He is Atticus Haygood Professor of Creative Writing and English at Emory University in Atlanta, Georgia.

RACHEL ZUCKER was born in New York in 1971. She is the author of three books of poetry: *The Bad Wife Handbook* (2007), *The Last Clear Narrative* (2004), and *Eating in the Underworld* (2003). She is a certified labor doula and lives in New York City.

PERMISSIONS

Lilah Hegnauer, "Teach Anything," "Katende Passion Fruit and Groundnuts," and "Immunizing in Bukoba" from *Dark Under Kiganda Stars*. Copyright © 2005 by Lilah Hegnauer. Reprinted with the permission of Ausable Press.

Honorée Fanonne Jeffers, "The Gospel of Barbecue" from *The Gospel of Barbecue*. Copyright © 2000 by Honorée Fanonne Jeffers. Reprinted with the permission of The Kent State University Press. "Outlandish Blues (The Movie)" and "Unidentified Female Student, Former Slave (Talladega College, circa 1885)" from *Outlandish Blues*. Copyright © 2003 by Honorée Fanonne Jeffers. Reprinted with the permission of Wesleyan University Press.

Devin Johnston, "Faces" from *Telepathy* (Paper Bark Press, 2001). "Los Angeles" and "The Life of Wood" from *Aversions* (Omnidawn, 2004). All reprinted by permission of the author.

Bhanu Kapil, 28 ["Where did you come from / how did you arrive?"], 48 ["What are the consequences of silence?"], 72 ["What are the consequences of silence?"], and 97 ["Who is responsible for the suffering of your mother?"] from *The Vertical Interrogation of Strangers*. Copyright © 2001 by Bhanu Kapil. Reprinted with the permission of Kelsey Street Press.

David Keplinger, "The Distance between Zero and One." Reprinted with the permission of the author. "Towards a Reconciliation with Disorder" and "Basic Training" from *The Clearing*. Copyright © 2005 by David Keplinger. Reprinted with the permission of New Issues Poetry & Prose.

Ben Lerner, "Your child lacks a credible god-term . . ." and "The sky narrates snow . . ." from *The Lichtenberg Figures*. Copyright © 2004 by Ben Lerner. "When night falls in the middle west" from *Angle of Yaw*. Copyright © 2006 by Ben Lerner. All reprinted with the permission of Copper Canyon Press, www.coppercanyonpress.org.

William Meredith, "The Illiterate" from *Effort at Speech: New and Selected Poems*. Copyright © 1997 by William Meredith. Reprinted with the permission of the author and Tri-Quarterly Books/Northwestern University Press.

Aimee Nezhukumatathil, "Gulabjamoon Jar," "Crow Joy," and "Making Gyotaku" from *Miracle Fruit*. Copyright © 2003 by Aimee Nezhukumatathil. All rights reserved. Reprinted with the permission of Tupelo Press.

Lisa Olstein, "Blue Warp Black Weave," "Another Story with a Burning Barn in It," and "Steady Now" from *Radio Crackling, Radio Gone*. Copyright © 2006 by Lisa Olstein. Reprinted with the permission of Copper Canyon Press, www.coppercanyonpress.org.

Diane Thiel, "Memento Mori in Middle School" and "Echolocations" from *Echolocations* (Ashland, Or.: Story Line Press, 2000). Copyright © 2000 by Diane Thiel. "Iphigeneia (Sapphics from Tauris)" from *Resistance Fantasies* (Ashland, Or.: Story Line Press, 2004). Copyright © 2004 by Diane Thiel. All reprinted with the permission of the author.

Natasha Trethewey, "Letter Home," "Letters from Storyville: December 1910," and "Storyville Diary: Bellocq" from *Bellocq's Ophelia: Poems*. Copyright © 2002 by Natasha Trethewey. Reprinted with the permission of Graywolf Press, Saint Paul, Minnesota.

Katrina Vandenberg, "The Floating," "Marriage Portrait of the Arnolfinis," and "Hunger Winter" from *Atlas: Poems*. Copyright © 2004 by Katrina Vandenberg. Reprinted with the permission of Milkweed Editions, www.milkweed.org.

Christian Wiman, "Clearing" from *The Long Home* (Ashland, Ore.: Story Line Press, 1998). Copyright © 1998 by Christian Wiman. Reprinted with the permission of the author. "Poštolka" and "Reading Herodotus" from *Hard Night*. Copyright © 2005 by Christian Wiman. Reprinted with the permission of Copper Canyon Press, www.coppercanyonpress.org.

Kevin Young, "Reward" and "Southern University, 1962" from *Most Way Home*. Copyright © 1995 by Kevin Young. Reprinted with the permission of HarperCollins Publishers. "Evensong" from *Jelly Roll: A Blues*. Copyright © 2003 by Kevin Young. Reprinted with the permission of Alfred A. Knopf, a division of Random House, Inc.

Rachel Zucker, "Letter [Persephone to Demeter]" from *Eating in the Underworld*. Copyright © 2003 by Rachel Zucker. "Thistle, or Letter for My Husband (33 Weeks)" and "The Desserts Will Make You Stupid with Happiness" from *The Last Clear Narrative*. Copyright © 2004 by Rachel Zucker. All reprinted with the permission of Wesleyan University Press.